AF350526

Train *to* Lead

THE UNSTOPPABLE LEADER'S PLAN FOR PEAK PERFORMANCE

CHRISTIAN MUNTEAN

Copyright © 2024 Christian Muntean

All rights reserved. No part of this publication may be reproduced, distributed, or transmitted in any form or by any means, including photocopying, recording, or other electronic or mechanical methods, without the prior written permission of the publisher, except in the case of brief quotations embodied in critical reviews and certain other noncommercial uses permitted by copyright law. For permission requests, write to the publisher, addressed "Attention: Permissions Coordinator," at the address below.

Oribi Press
6921 Brayton Drive Suite 204
Anchorage, AK 99507 USA

ISBN: 979-8-218-32238-0 (paperback)
ISBN: 979-8-9900981-0-7 (ebook)
ISBN: 979-8-9900981-1-4 (hardcover)
ISBN: 979-8-9900981-2-1 (audiobook)

Library of Congress Control Number: 2024905689

Ordering Information:
Special discounts are available on quantity purchases by corporations, associations, and others. For details, contact christian@christianmuntean.com, www.christianmuntean.com, (907) 522-7200

Publisher's Cataloging-in-Publication Data
Names: Muntean, Christian, 1974- .
Title: Train to lead : The unstoppable leader's plan for peak performance / Christian Muntean.
Description: Anchorage, AK : Oribi Press, 2024. | Includes bibliographic references. | Includes 2 charts and 1 diagram. | Summary: Outlines a proven method for enhancing leadership abilities, drawing parallels between athletic training and leadership development. With exercises and practical examples, it targets both new and seasoned leaders, aiming to refine their skills for peak performance.
Identifiers: LCCN 2024905689 | ISBN 9798990098107 (hardcover) | ISBN 9798218322380 (pbk.) | ISBN 9798990098114 (ebook) | ISBN 9798990098121 (audiobook)
Subjects: LCSH: Leadership. | Mentoring. | Executive coaching. | BISAC: BUSINESS & ECONOMICS / Leadership. | BUSINESS & ECONOMICS / Mentoring & Coaching. | SELF-HELP / Personal Growth / Success.
Classification: LCC HD57.7 M86 2024 | DDC 658/092--dc23LC record available at https://lccn.loc.gov/2024905689

ACKNOWLEDGEMENTS

Many, many individuals and organizations have gone out of their way to invest in my growth as a leader over the years. (Maybe I looked like I needed that much help?)

There is no way I can thank everyone. But I want to acknowledge some who played key roles in my path to here: David Wangaard and Judith Green, you both worked with very raw material and helped me develop my early bearings. Carter Eby for second chances and including me in the Bonhoeffer's Espresso startup. Rick Benjamin, for being encouraging and making room. Bruce Bauman and Harry Tees for trusting I could handle being over my head. Jim Richardson for being a matchless mentor. Medair, for trusting me to meet the challenge and offering my first opportunity to attend a formal leadership training. Eastern University for going to bat for me. Sid Buzzell who, probably unknowingly, helped guide me through a very long, very dark night of the soul. Brian Green for taking me in, giving me room to sort out my stuff and providing me with a launch pad. Tim Gravel whose generosity gave me room to figure things out. The M.J. Murdock Charitable Trust who included me in the Mentoring Experience and introduced me to fantastic people. One of those was Walt Wright whose thinking and approach to leadership has shaped much of my own. Gwen Kennedy, who was very generous to me, and the first professional example of what I was trying to become. Alan Weiss, who forced me to get in or get out. (I got in.) Craig Ballantyne, who has become an important sounding board and an example of 'going for it' without losing perspective.

And, of course, my wife Marta. She has softened many of my rough edges and offers perspective and wisdom when I need it. Finally, Jesus Christ, who is an example to me, and shapes how I understand leadership and try to relate to others.

As I look back through this list, the people who helped me the most were examples in their own lives, saw potential, made room for messiness and included me in what they were doing. They helped me grow as a person. That is what helped me become a better leader.

As a former fitness expert, competitive athlete, and now entrepreneur and author, I've read hundreds of books about exercise science, muscle growth, and leadership. Often, the books on exercise science are too nerdy for the common person, and the so-called leadership books are often biographies of good people who were in the right place in the right industry at the right time.

I'd never read a book that covers leadership growth science in a way that's practical. And the reason there had never been a book like this before is because no one had ever adequately assessed how to create leaders in a systematic way.

We—meaning larger corporations and entrepreneurs like myself—often assume that sending our people to motivational events or giving them textbooks on how to run meetings will be enough for passing along the skills of leadership. But that's the wrong approach (as I've learned the hard way).

I agree with Christian that what's missing from the leadership library is a program—one that can show a leader at any stage of their development how to get to the next level of elite leadership.

What the world of leadership needs is a new, improved, holistic approach to building good people into leaders from the ground up, in much the same way that personal trainers and strength coaches contribute to the creation of athletic champions. In fact, there are many parallels between the sports and fitness world and that of leadership. That's why many people claim virtue in sports participation and so many good leaders have a high-performance background.

In both worlds—athletics and leadership—success is simple but not easy. It requires dedication, willpower, self-discipline, and perhaps most importantly, humility—admitting we don't know everything and asking for help.

If you're a leader, or if you want to help grow your team of leaders, this book is one of the most important places to begin.

I wish this approach had been available to me in my own career as my role changed from personal trainer to solo entrepreneur to leader of a team of dozens of hard-working people who depended on me to guide them.

I skipped over the basics that Christian begins with. I didn't think of building my foundation until years after I had accumulated bad habits in the basics. Christian's unique periodization approach would have fixed that for me, and that's why I know it's so important that everyone start there—no matter how much experience they have.

As I look around at my entrepreneur friends, I can tell which ones were somehow able to adopt a similar approach to their leadership growth as the process Christian outlines in this "training manual." Still, I know they would have achieved their leadership success faster had they had access to this book—which is truly Christian's lifework.

If you're ready to work smarter and not harder, if you're ready to step into your greatness as a leader or build a championship team of leaders, then take the *Train to Lead* mindset seriously.

It's the missing link in leadership today.

Craig Ballantyne
Author, *Perfect Week Formula*
Owner, EarlytoRise.com

Many years ago, a friend challenged me to run a half-marathon with her. I wouldn't consider myself a runner, but I ran cross-country in high school, and I have mixed running into my training on and off over the years. I figured if she could run a half-marathon, so could I.

She sent me her training plan. I looked at it and ignored it. If you want to run a long way, just run a long way. Do it over and over again, and it gets easier. How complicated is that? I didn't need a plan.

Or so I thought.

I started running a lot. In old shoes. I got the miles in—many more than her plan called for, because I was better than the plan.

Then my hip started to hurt. It would hurt so badly that I was no longer able to complete training runs. But even then I didn't realize that my ability to "gut it out" didn't match my body's ability to adapt to repetitive stress.

I didn't know how to train. I didn't give myself time to build up. I figured that recovery was for wimps. Decent shoes were a waste of money.

I ended up having to settle for a 5K. This was the distance I could tolerate before my hip would seize up. I completed the race, but that's about all I can say about my performance.

As it turned out, there is more to running than just running.

There is more to leadership than just being called a leader.

Most leaders end up becoming leaders for reasons other than knowing how to lead. If you are like them, you've probably already achieved some level of professional success or competency. But then a circumstance arises—a situation where you realize, "I don't know how to handle this."

For many leaders, a team conflict triggers this kind of situation. Or the organization begins to grow quickly and becomes more complex. Or there is crisis. Or there's an opportunity that requires some risk. Leadership is needed when the way forward is unclear. When results aren't guaranteed. When risk is a companion. When leadership is most needed, many leaders discover they aren't sure what to do.

The path into leadership is often a mysterious one.

The role of "leader" is the role of greatest impact in any organization. In spite of this, most leaders have never been taught how to lead. In most cases, leadership skill wasn't even a criterion for the role. Leaders are often promoted to leadership due to their professional excellence and reputation, or an ability to sell, or longevity, or because they are trusted and responsible. Many others are entrepreneurs who built the position themselves. Or they were moved into a leadership position because of a relational decision based on family, familiarity, or politics.

Most leaders don't become leaders because of their leadership knowledge or skill. And in fact, most people who hire leaders aren't even sure how to evaluate whether a leader knows how to lead. This explains the statistic that roughly two-thirds of all leadership successions fail. This number improves only to a one-third failure rate for Fortune 200 companies, which is better. But it still demonstrates the one-in-three odds that some of the best and brightest leaders and boards in the country will get it wrong.

The basic assumption about leadership (similar to my assumption about running) is often "just do it." What "it" is or how to do it is usually poorly defined.

So how do you learn to lead?

I grew up playing sports, but I never paid attention to training approaches. Coaches just told me what to do. I didn't think about it. I cut corners when I could.

My half-marathon experience was an eye-opener for me. I discovered there was more to running well than just showing up and trying really hard. There was definitely more than just thinking, "If *she* can do it, I can definitely do it."

I had run cross-country and track and field in high school, so I wasn't inexperienced, but I had never designed my own training plans. I just did what the coach said. Following my half-marathon experience, I became interested in the how-tos of fitness and athletics. This led to a 12-year hobby as a strength and conditioning instructor.

After many years, in my late 40s, I started competing in amateur athletic events again—specifically Brazilian jiu-jitsu. Now I know how to train. I feel better and I feel ready. I don't make fun of training plans anymore. If I don't know how to train for something new, I work with a coach or pay for a plan.

The science around fitness and athletic performance is fascinating to me. One of the most interesting things I've learned is that it's possible to train for and produce predictable results within a given time frame. I've trained mountaineers for successful climbs to the highest peaks, soldiers for mountain warfare, endurance athletes for corrective strength and mobility, and deconditioned desk jockeys for weight loss and rediscovery of the freedom of movement.

The training programs I designed reliably achieved predictable results.

One day as I was heading home from the gym, I realized that the leadership world *does not* have this kind of track record. Yes, there are enormous numbers of leadership books as well as training programs and materials available, but most of them take a scattershot approach. "Here's a bunch of leadership ideas! Try one! Try them all!" That's not too different from grabbing a random "lose weight now" or "look like this movie star in six weeks" workout from the internet and hoping it will help you prepare for your specific goals.

Other books are very narrowly focused and very well researched. They might be on habits, or strategy, or scaling up, or emotional intelligence. But when should you use that information? How does it apply in your context—along with everything else that you need to do? Basically, how do all these great ideas work together? (And should they?)

By no means am I discounting the value of other outlooks. The topics I've referred to above are useful—some are even critical for success as a leader. Their value is not the issue. The issue is figuring out how to apply the information out there without getting overly focused on less important concepts or becoming overwhelmed by all the concepts. How do all the pieces fit together?

Train to Lead is designed to be like having a coach. Helping you know what to focus on and when.

MY PHILOSOPHY OF LEADERSHIP

*The servant-leader is servant first, it begins with a natural feeling
that one wants to serve, to serve first, as opposed to wanting
power, influence, fame, or wealth.* — Robert Greenleaf[1]

Servant leadership provides the philosophical underpinnings of this book. The essence of servant leadership is that a leader should be primarily motivated by a desire to serve the interests of someone else: the customer, the employees, the community, the shareholders, etc. This is in contrast to leader-first approaches. The essence of leader-first leadership is that the interests, vision, or goals of the leader come first. The interests of others aren't necessarily disregarded, but they are subordinate to those of the leader.

The term "servant leader" was coined by Robert Greenleaf in 1970;[2] however, the concept of servant leadership wasn't created by him. It has existed for thousands of years across cultures.[3]

Greenleaf worked for AT&T, which at the time was the world's largest company. It was there that he began researching leadership and management, and he later went on to consult with institutions such as MIT and

Lilly Endowment Inc.[4] Part of his focus was on trying to understand not just how leaders should lead but *why anyone would follow.*

In the 1960s and '70s, perhaps like now, there was a great degree of social upheaval and distrust in authority. Greenleaf wondered what would allow people who distrusted authority to accept someone as a leader. His observation was that people voluntarily follow a leader when they feel their interests are or will be served by that leader.

Many leaders trying to accrue support know that they need to appeal to the interests of others—just follow any political campaign to see that— but it also extends to the corporate office or warehouse floor. Although many leaders use the language of service to support their own goals, once we set rhetoric aside and observe actual decisions and actions, we discover that only some leaders actually are primarily motivated by serving others.

It's not always easy to differentiate between the two. We can't see someone else's motivation, and it can even be difficult to be honest about or to discern our own. Motivations can shift over time, and they exist on a spectrum. Leaders aren't purely "other-" or "self-motivated." There's always a little of both, though some tend to lean more toward their own interests and some toward the interests of others.

Also, and this is important, our own interests aren't innately wrong or lesser than. It's not wrong to have a vision, goals, or desires. The difference is about how we relate to others.

To differentiate between the two, look at impact. Robert Greenleaf offered this test:

"Do those being served grow as persons; do they, while being served, become healthier, wiser, freer, more autonomous, more likely themselves to become servants? And what is the effect on the least privileged in society; will she or he benefit, or, at least, not be further deprived?"[5]

The language of this quote can feel very idealistic—perhaps more appropriate for a nonprofit than a business. But apply it to a common challenge for new leaders: learning to build a team and delegate.

Many leaders have a tendency to struggle with trust, impatience, or perfectionism (often concerned about how a job will reflect on them). In other cases, leaders simply aren't organized well enough to know how to delegate. As a result, they hold onto decision-making information and authority, requiring others to come to them for permission.

But a leader can flip the script from "How can I succeed when I have to manage all these people?" to "How do I help all of these people grow so we can accomplish our goals?" This is a shift toward servant leadership. And it produces more effective leaders and teams.

While some leader-first leaders use the language of servant leadership, their actions will tend toward using rather than growing others. It often shows up in workplaces with a high level of internal drama, soap-opera politics, and so on. And it is often correlated with issues such as high turn-over rates, customer complaints, and internal and external conflict.

It's not that leader-first leadership doesn't work. It does—depending on how you define "work." Pick your favorite despot—something is working for them. But, at best, that approach to leadership uses people, and at worst, it hurts them. Leader-first leaders often spend much more time and many more resources attempting to maintain control and far less time simply providing value.

That being said, just being motivated to serve doesn't mean that you'll be effective as a leader—there are stacks of well-motivated people accomplishing little to nothing. If you truly want to lead well, you have to also be committed to growth.

All of that being said, the premise of this book assumes the reader's interest in servant leadership. My recommendations are rooted in that perspective.

HOW THIS BOOK IS STRUCTURED

I patterned this book on the fitness principles of periodization, a training approach that breaks a large training goal into focused training segments. A set amount of time—usually between two and six weeks—is spent within each focus, then the athlete moves on to the next, with each segment building on the previous. It's a well-established and effective training approach in the fitness world.[6]

As a consultant and coach, I started to apply this approach to my leadership development clients. It worked. Within a relatively short period of time, I'd see repeatable patterns of growth. I was onto something.

Here's the core application concept: Leadership, like fitness, requires ongoing work. You can't "get fit" and hold on to that accomplishment for the rest of your life. You have to keep at it. Leadership is similar. It's something you build and maintain and can constantly improve.

This book is built on six sections. Each of which builds on the previous.

HEALTHY HABITS: IN WITH THE GOOD, OUT WITH THE BAD

Just as good nutrition is the foundation of fitness, good habits are the foundation of effective leadership.

As the familiar saying goes, "You can't outrun a donut." Broadly speaking, how we eat and sleep has a significant impact on our physical health and performance. Here's another old fitness saying: "Six pack abs are made in the kitchen."

Unless we change our basic nutritional habits, most fitness goals are difficult to achieve and impossible to sustain. This is true for leadership as well. We've all accumulated behaviors, habits, and mindsets that either support our success as leaders or work against it. Some of those habits and mindsets need to be changed or dropped. Others need to be added.

This section doesn't focus on leadership. It prepares for that. But many leaders experience dramatic growth just by making these changes.

CONDITIONING: BUILDING YOUR PLATFORM

This section introduces the basic self-management practices that leaders need to develop to be able to lead and manage others well.

Physical training is by definition stressful. Leadership is often stressful as well. Conditioning is the work that needs to be done to prepare your body to be able to take on and manage additional stress without injury.

In modern society, many people are physically deconditioned. Before they can meaningfully train for a sport or fitness goal, they first need to develop a base level of conditioning. Skipping this step often causes burnout or injury (like I did with my hip in trying to run without a training program).

Even experienced leaders need to condition for a significant change; the shift from leading a stable company to a fast-growth company can be a shock to the system. The majority of my executive coaching clients—who are already senior leaders—need to go back and work on the fundamentals of conditioning.

STRENGTH: MAKING THINGS HAPPEN

In this section, I will introduce you to the five necessary strengths of leadership and how to build them.

Strength is simply defined as the ability to exert force to create or resist movement. Leaders are almost defined by their ability to make something happen or to ensure that certain things *don't* happen. This is strength.

POWER: DECISIVENESS, SPEED, AND MOMENTUM

This section explores when and how to exercise power in your leadership.

Power is the ability to exert strength quickly and in a way that generates momentum. Being strong isn't enough. There are times when leaders need to create movement in difficult situations or force a change in direction. This is particularly true during times of conflict, change or crisis.

I can stand up from a chair, but can I also jump from a seated position? The difference is power. Power requires strength and adds speed. At times, leaders need to act powerfully: quickly, decisively, and effectively.

ENDURANCE: STAYING WITH IT OVER THE LONG HAUL

This section introduces perspectives and habits that will help you stay in the game over time.

Endurance is the ability to maintain a consistent level of output over a long duration. In athletics, it's easy to "gas out" or develop injuries due to being unprepared for the long haul. A big part of endurance is mental toughness—building the ability to dig deep and find those hidden reserves.

In leadership, it often takes time to see your desired results, and there are difficult times when it's all too easy to want to simply walk away. Most leaders fail because they lack the ability to endure long enough to see success come in.

RECOVERY: WHERE TRUE GROWTH HAPPENS

This section introduces self-maintenance and recovery and how both are necessary to build your leadership and life.

Self-maintenance and recovery are vital for sustaining leadership effectiveness and personal well-being. Like athletes who grow stronger during rest after stressing their bodies, leaders too must incorporate downtime into their routines. Effective rest and recovery not only prevent burnout but also foster resilience, mental clarity, and long-term health. Embracing rest is crucial for leaders to rejuvenate and achieve sustained success.

HOW TO USE THIS BOOK

This book is an overview of the necessary fundamentals for *being a leader*. At the end of the book, I offer three training plans that you can use to help guide your growth. Choose the plan that seems appropriate to you. Here are three recommendations that will help you maximize the value of the approach you choose:

Read it all: I recommend that everyone read—or at least skim—through the entire book. It'll give you an overview of how the topics fit together.

Start now: That being said, you don't need to read the entire book to start using it. You don't need to "master" a chapter or concept before you read on. In fact, you won't be able to. Focus on gaining familiarity with the concepts and making progress. Mastery comes with practice.

Focus on one section at a time: Don't try to work on everything all at once. Just as athletes cycle through different phases of training emphases, I encourage you to pick one section or even one specific topic to focus on for a time. A singular focus *doesn't* mean that you drop what you previously learned or developed. You wouldn't stop using strength just because you are focusing on endurance for a time. Similarly, don't drop good self-management habits because you are developing a new strength. But focus on one area of growth at a time.

EXERCISES AND PLANS

Putting It into Practice: Exercises

At the end of each chapter, I offer suggestions for practicing the concepts of the chapter. Just as reading a fitness book won't make you fit, reading a leadership book won't produce leadership. You have to do some work.

Some of my recommendations require dedicated time and attention. Many can be integrated into your normal business activities. I recommend setting some time aside weekly, even 15 minutes, to review your goals as well as when and how you will approach them.

Self-Assessment and Training Plans

At the end of the book, you will find an assessment that will help you understand where to focus your efforts. You can take that now. Additionally, there are three training plan options. You can use the results of your assessment to determine which plan seems the best option for you.

Train to Lead Journal: The Train to Lead Journal contains the Leadership Self-Assessment, training plans and all of the exercises in this book. It's the perfect place to track your reflections and progress.

Plus, it's free! Download it here: www.christianmuntean.com/train-to-lead-journal/

Ready to Get Started?

Turn the page, and we'll begin with a look at the foundational habits that health and high-impact leaders have in place.

HEALTHY HABITS: NUTRITION AND ENVIRONMENT

In with the good, out with the bad.

Dis-moi ce que tu manges, je te dirai ce que tu es.
[Tell me what you eat, and I will tell you what you are]
— Anthelme Brillat-Savarin, 1826[7]

CHAPTER 1

Introduction to Healthy Habits

Becoming or staying physically fit begins in what might seem like surprising places: *Outside* of the gym. *Off* the trails or treadmills. Fitness begins with how we live our daily lives: how we eat and drink, how we sleep, and even who we spend time with.

How we eat and drink provides our bodies with the raw materials to build health. If we eat and hydrate well, our bodies tend to do well. If we don't, our bodies don't.

How we sleep and rest gives our bodies time to heal and grow. If we practice good sleep and rest habits, our bodies do well.

While those two points probably don't come as a surprise, this one may: who we spend time with and the quality of that time *also* affect our physical health.

Since 1948, the Framingham Heart Study has tracked the cardiovascular health of families within the town of Framingham, Massachusetts, for three generations.[8] It has shown that both happiness and obesity (among other things) are affected by social networks and proximity. If someone you know becomes happy, there is a 25% greater chance that you will be happy.[9] If a friend becomes obese, there is a 57% chance you will as well.[10]

Many studies have shown that building and maintaining healthy, committed relationships influences our health. Some studies focus specifically on home life. Others focus on our wider circle of relationships. Either way, studies have shown that the quality of our relationships affects us physically and mentally:

- Stress levels. Stress causes our body to release cortisol and other stress hormones. Consistently high levels of stress are associated with many health factors.[11]
- Better healing. One study suggests that patients in long-term relationships are three times more likely to survive heart surgery than single patients.[12]
- Sense of purpose. A sense of purpose has been shown to reduce mortality risk.[13]
- Overall life span. One study shows that size of our social network was positively associated with life span.[14]

Our quality as leaders parallels this. Leadership effectiveness begins *outside* of where you lead. It begins with how you choose to live your daily life. This includes the influences you allow into your life, how you make space for growth, and who you spend time with.

And, frankly, your physical health also matters.

When it comes to leadership development, I repeat this refrain: "You lead out of who you are." Who you are is heavily influenced by the company you keep and the environments and perspectives you are exposed to. Growing up, we can't control this. But as adults—and especially as leaders—it becomes a responsibility to curate who we spend time with and what we expose ourselves to. The practice of doing so begins to shape the quality of the leadership we can provide.

Three Leadership Toxins: In with the Good, Out with the Bad

Leaders lead out of who they are. Because of this, it is an obligation of leadership that we continually work on ourselves. For leaders, personal development *is* leadership development.

Consider this:

Fearful or insecure leaders tend to be rigid or vacillating, defensive or indecisive. Angry leaders may be reactive, spiteful, or dominating. Depressed leaders may withdraw or be unpredictable.

Conversely, confident leaders are able both to set a clear direction and to welcome input that may alter the direction. Calm and reflective leaders are able to respond appropriately and with the right balance of engagement and authority. Resilient, positive leaders are able to engage challenges and disappointments as opportunities.

Healthy leadership is similar to physical wellness. To a large degree, we are products of what we eat and our environment. But sometimes it isn't just about getting more good in. It's about getting some of the bad, or toxic, out.

What are toxins for leaders? Toxins in the physical world are any substances that are harmful or poisonous to our health. Toxins for leaders are dynamics that are harmful or poisonous to our leadership and the relational contexts we lead in. There are many potential toxins, but three are common: your core story and beliefs, your relationships, and your habits.

Toxin #1: Your Core Story

By "core story," I mean the narrative that influences or directs your life. We all have one. This is the "deep" story that we believe we are part of. For most of us, it developed out of the thousands of repeated experiences and messages that formed our sense of who we are. For some of us, there are specific, significant incidents that shaped our perspectives.

Either way, this sense of "who I am" and "how I fit" continues to guide or influence our behavior. Your story could be tied to your family, faith, school experiences, social class, ethnicity, gender, or any number of other things. In most situations, the stories we are living are primarily reactive to experiences in the past, and because they are reactive, we tend to recreate aspects or components of them. This contributes to a self-perpetuation of the stories or those experiences, which are good when the story is good.

But if our stories still cause us to react in ways that no longer serve us well, they become toxic. They make us sick—for example, if I grew up feeling as if I wasn't allowed to make a mistake, it may cause a level of perfectionism that inhibits decision-making. It may make it difficult to trust and delegate effectively to others. Perfectionism, ironically, is a great inhibitor of growth and success.

If I grew up feeling financially insecure or that resources were always scarce, I might become too risk averse. This could cause me to struggle to recognize and pursue opportunities. It might make it difficult for me to make long-term investments financially or relationally. It might also make me suspicious of the success of others, especially if I believe that their success means there is less "pie" available for everyone else.

Clients, especially my entrepreneurial clients, often confide in me that part of their drive to succeed comes from wanting to prove something to someone else. It could be a parent or a former business partner or spouse.

Too often, they are trying to prove something to someone who is already dead or isn't paying attention.

So, what does a leader do? If they want to be healthy, they detox.
Walter Wright of the Max De Pree Center for Leadership says that our core beliefs shape our character.[15] Character shapes our values. Our values form our relationships. Our relationships inform our behavior. Our behavior leads to whether or not we (as leaders) create cultures where others can thrive. If we do, this leads to profits, success in goals, etc.

Our lives and identities are formed by the narratives we tell ourselves. By examining and rewriting these narratives, we can change our core beliefs and shape our own lives.

The following exercise uses your story to help you uncover and change your core beliefs.

Materials Needed
- A quiet space
- Pen and paper or a digital device for writing
- A reflective attitude

Steps

1. Reflect.

Take a few minutes to center yourself. Take deep breaths, and try to clear your mind.

2. Outline your life story.

Outline your life story as you see it now. Keep it brief; try not to go beyond one page. Focus on the major highlights or lowlights that stand out to you and have shaped who you are. The goal is to get you thinking, not to write an autobiography!

If you find yourself getting stuck, set a timer for 20 minutes and force yourself to complete this step by then.

3. *Identify core beliefs.*

Reread your outline. Underline or highlight moments or statements that shaped your core beliefs. These might be beliefs about God, yourself, other people, or the world in general. Make a note of what those beliefs are.

4. *Characterize your beliefs.*

Imagine that your core beliefs are characters in your story. Give each belief a name, a personality, and a role in your story—for example, if I have a belief that I can't make mistakes, I might name this character "Perfect Christian."

5. *Examine the characters.*

For each character, ask yourself:
- What role has this character played in my story?
- How has this character influenced my emotions and decisions?
- Has this character been helpful or harmful?

6. *Identify turning points.*

Look at your life story, and identify any turning points or significant events. How did your characters (core beliefs) react or change during these times?

7. *Revise your story.*

Consider how you want your story to evolve. Are there characters you want to transform or write out of your story?

For the characters you want to change, think of ways they can evolve. For instance, Perfect Christian could become Effective Christian, reflecting a belief that effectiveness is more important than perfection.

Imagine a version of your future life story that incorporates these changes. What are the major highlights and possible challenges you may encounter?

8.   Visualize your new story.

Close your eyes and visualize your life as it unfolds according to your new story. Imagine how the evolved characters influence your decisions, relationships, and well-being.

9.   Create a plan.

Write down steps you can take to make this new story a reality. This can include new habits and thought patterns or seeking support from friends, a coach, or a therapist. Most importantly, what is the one thing you need to do to start?

10. Reflect regularly.

Set aside time each week to reflect on your new story and how it is shaping your life. Make adjustments as necessary to stay aligned with your desired narrative. Personally, I read a short version of this every morning.

11. Evaluate.

After a month of living your new story, write a brief reflection on how this exercise has affected your core beliefs and your life.

Remember that you are the author of your own life story. Through reflection and intentional action, you have the power to change your narrative and, in doing so, transform your core beliefs and your life. I'm a person of faith, so I find it helpful to be prayerful in exercises like this. It isn't necessary, but you may choose to do so as well.

You don't have to complete this step before moving on, but you will find that any work you do in this space will help you move forward more quickly and address issues or habits that "block" your success. And there is another side benefit of this exercise: A major leadership function is to define and interpret reality. To a large degree, leaders determine reality for their teams. They define what is an opportunity or a threat. They differentiate between potential friends or foes.

Toxin #2: Unhelpful Relationships

You may have heard the quote by motivational speaker Jim Rohn, "You are the average of the five closest people you surround yourself with." It's a compelling thought, and for many purposes it is true enough. However, as the Framingham Heart Study suggests that we are actually the sum of a much larger network of relationships *including people we've never met.*

We can't control the full extent of our social network, but as adults, we usually have a lot of influence over our immediate relationships.

- Am I surrounding myself with the kinds of people I'd like to become?
- Are my primary relationships with people who are creating, encouraging, growing, and building the kinds of lives that I aspire to?

Cleanse. Effective leaders are intentional and intentionally surround themselves with good, motivational friends, family, and mentors. Some leaders who are effective but isolated will find themselves experiencing either burnout or the accumulated consequences of poor judgment.

It's sad to see how many late-career leaders fail to "end well." In almost every instance, you'll find a leader who has isolated themselves from strong, healthy peers who are willing to encourage and challenge them.

My career and life reached an inflection point when I did the following exercise. I noticed that most of my closest relationships were with guys I liked but who were unambitious in their careers, tended to complain about their relationships, didn't put a lot of effort into their physical health, or didn't seem encouraging spiritually.

I started to spend much less time with them and began to seek out friends, mentors, and coaches who were ambitious professionally, who were positive and intentional about their marriages and families, who put effort into their health, and who seemed to be able to encourage and challenge me spiritually. Not everyone ticked every box, but in general they did.

That shift changed my life.

Take a Relationship Inventory
- What are your highest values and goals?
- What do you hope for in terms of personal, professional, relational, financial, or spiritual development?
- What growth or support do you need to live out your new story (above) for your future?
- Reflect on your current closest relationships:
  - Who challenges you to live out your values and toward your goals?
  - Who is stagnant or stalled in life or their profession?
  - Which ones live in ways that are contrary to who you want to become?
  - Is there anyone you should spend more time with?
  - Is there anyone you should spend less time with?
- What relationships are you missing that you need in your life? This may include friends and colleagues as well as mentors, coaches, or therapists.

If you hope to move to the next level in leadership, you need to ensure your relationships are with "next-level" people. If you want to sustain effective, influential leadership over the long haul, you'll need to spend time with people who are healthy and pull you forward. I'll address this at greater depth in the next chapter.

Toxin #3: Unhelpful Habits
Unhelpful habits are lifestyle choices that do not contribute to—or that consume energy or bandwidth or detract from—health. They may be as simple as poor energy/priority/time management and organizational disciplines. They may be as personal as poor sleeping and eating habits, which prevent us from operating at our best during the day. They may extend to addictive behaviors and self-medication. Either way, we all tend to develop patterns of behavior that don't serve us well.

The best leaders *actively architect* their habits. They understand that good habits propel succession. Poor habits either divert from success or actively undermine it. In study after study of high-performing leaders, you see a clear pattern of intentional discipline around personal habits.

What are the top one or two habits that come to mind for you that you might want to change? If I were to ask your spouse or close friend or colleague, what might they say?

HABIT CHANGE EXERCISE

As executive coach Marshall Goldsmith has observed, "What got you here won't get you there."[16] Changing behaviors can be difficult. And it is, in fact, a physical (neurological) activity. Our habits are essentially programs that our brain has learned and has wired in. We no longer have to think about what we want to do. When a cue occurs, the program kicks in.

Working on the first two toxins is enormously helpful when it comes to changing habits. Becoming aware of and rewriting your story or your identity is critical, as is surrounding yourself with relationships and influences that support the new habits you want to build.

In his book *Atomic Habits,* James Clear breaks habits into four stages: Cue > Craving > Response > Reward[17]

Cue: the trigger
Craving: the feeling the trigger generates
Response: how we act to address the craving
Reward: the benefit that we receive from the response

A healthy habit is one that generates positive, constructive consequences to our responses:

Cue: Monday morning, I arrive at the office.
Craving: I feel disoriented about the week to come and a little overwhelmed because of how full my calendar is.
Response: I sit down, write a list of what I need to accomplish, and I identify the one most important goal for the week and the one goal for the day.

Reward: I feel focused and calm.

Consequences: I'm more productive, I'm on time with projects, and I feel a sense of accomplishment overall.

An unhealthy habit is one that generates negative, unwanted consequences to our responses:

Cue: I arrive home after a long, stressful day at work.

Craving: I need to de-stress and relax.

Response: I pour my first double bourbon for the night.

Reward: Some of the tension starts to melt away.

Consequences: My double bourbon is followed by another. I'm not getting wasted, but I am putting on the pounds. My sleep quality goes down. I wake up feeling less energetic and less focused.

To change a habit, we need to change either or both the cue or the response, as in the example below:

Cue: I arrive home after a long, stressful day at work.

Craving: I need to de-stress and relax.

New Response: I take the dog for a walk when I get home.

Reward: Some of the tension has melted away.

Consequences: I feel able to shift gears and engage with the family. I sleep well and wake up refreshed. I'm happy with what I see on the scale.

It's often critical to change the cue as well. If every day is long and stressful, it's helpful to look back into the day and determine what you can control that will reduce either the length or the stress.

Nearly all of the executives I work with struggle with priorities, stress, energy, and time management. They commonly come back to me after we've worked together for a while and say, "My home life has dramatically improved as a result of our work together! My spouse loves what you are doing with me!" This is simply because the work we do that helps them be more focused and productive during the day translates into removing or reducing stress-inducing cues. In the past, those old cues would send them down the path of unhelpful habit patterns.

For most people, it's easier to go to the gym than it is to have a disciplined and healthy diet. Both have value for health: If you want to be an athlete you have to train, but if you don't eat well, you will undermine the benefits of training. Leaders who learn the skills of leadership without building a healthy lifestyle will struggle with more burnout, health issues, family issues, and so on. You lead out of who you are.

Finally, the three leadership toxins that we've discussed in this chapter are not easy to address for most people. But you can address them. If you find yourself stuck working on your own, get help. I have worked with many clients who have made radical changes within six months to a year. When they do, it has had holistic, broad benefits. Work and life get better. My clients become more effective leaders, and they haven't even gotten into working on specific leadership abilities yet …

Putting It into Practice: Exercises
- What is one toxin that you need to address?
- What specific steps will you take to address it?
- When will you do this?
- What support do you need?

CHAPTER 3

How I See Myself: The Starting Point

Once, while I led a fitness class, a new attendee slipped into the back. He was a big guy with well-developed "peacock" muscles. These are muscles that look good but aren't necessarily strong.

The focus of my class that day had to do with stabilizer muscles and compound movements. Many of the exercises were atypical and challenging. The new guy worked out with us for a while but struggled to keep up.

Many athletes actually love discovering a new challenge like this. That was part of the reason my class attracted so many elite athletes. They take a search-and-destroy attitude toward personal limitations. High-performing athletes like being pushed. I hoped that this would be the new guy's response. Instead, after about 15 or 20 minutes of trying and failing to keep up with the group, he quit. He walked to the other side of the gym where the bench press was set up. Immediately, he began to crank out heavy sets on the bench.

Who knows what he was actually thinking, but to me it appeared he was used to being the biggest and strongest person in the room. When he found a situation that challenged that identity, he left it and moved to where he was comfortable and could look good. I might be mistaken, but I think it was his self-image rather than his not having a strong kinetic chain that was holding him back.

When I began working with leaders, I assumed that most of my work would focus on practical or strategic topics. But I discovered that most leaders wrestle with self-image issues—specifically, limiting decisions and behaviors that stem from their self-image.

As a result, it is a leadership responsibility to actively cultivate a healthy self-image.

Here is how that works:

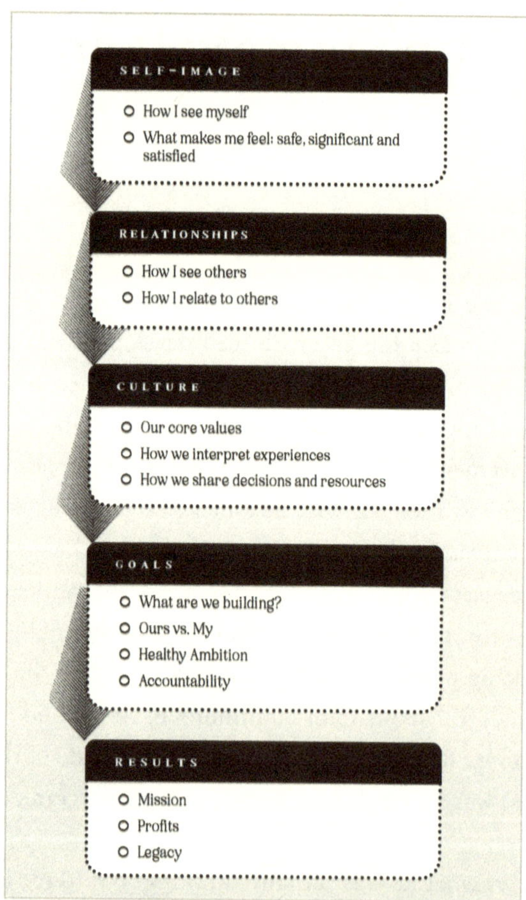

How self-image drives a leader's results

How I see myself affects how I see other people and relate to them.

Consider two driven leaders: One leader is a high-performer but is often perfectionistic and demanding of those around them. This leader may say, "I'm the hardest on myself." They may be right, but that doesn't mitigate the impact of the impractically high standards they set for others.

This behavior is often related to tying performance to personal value. This leader may believe that to be accepted or "good enough" they must also be perfect or some form of "the best." Because they know they aren't perfect, they are hard on themselves, but they may also be critical and difficult with everyone else.

Contrast this with an ambitious and motivated leader who understands that mistakes are part of the learning curve. This leader drives for performance but doesn't tie it to personal value. Their sense of worth or value is rooted elsewhere. While requiring results, this leader tends to have tolerance and offers support for the growth journeys of others.

Each approach affects and informs relationships. The patterns of those relationships create a culture. This culture defines and reinforces how a team relates to one another, how individual and group experiences are understood, and how decisions are made. All of this shapes the environment for goal-setting and pursuit, which leads to the quality of the results that can be achieved.

Over time, aspects of the personality and relational behaviors of the senior leader will be reflected throughout an organization. In many cases, simply by observing a sampling of frontline teams it's possible to describe likely characteristics of executive teams.

There is an old proverb that says, "A tree is judged by its fruit." In other words, looking at the tree doesn't necessarily tell you if it is healthy, but looking at its fruit will. If the results we're getting in an organization aren't what we want, it's worth looking at the source, which is often the leader. And the leader has been shaped by their self-image.

CHANGING SELF-IMAGE

Fortunately, we can change how we see ourselves.

Exercise 1: Change Your Mirrors

> *The thing that moves us to pride or shame is not the mere mechanical reflection of ourselves but the imagined effect of this reflection upon another's mind.* — Charles Horton Cooley[18]

Charles Cooley was an early sociologist. He noticed that, as children, we develop our sense of identity based on how others relate to us. In other words, we see ourselves in the mirror of other people.[19]

It gets tricky though: Our *interpretation* of how others see us influences us more than how others actually do see us. It works like this: We are surrounded by other people. We imagine how we must appear to them. We imagine the judgments they make about us (affirmative or negative). We develop our self-image based on *how we believe we are judged.*

When written out like this, it's easy to see the subjectivity of our self-image. It's very open to interpretation.

If we want to change our self-identity, we need to change those mirrors. This nearly always includes changing who we surround ourselves with. It may also include gaining a more accurate sense of how people actually experience us.

This brings relationships up again. I mention our relationships because improving those is often the most difficult step. It's also the one that will have the greatest impact.

Many leaders still see themselves in the mirrors of people they were surrounded by in the past. For some of us, this was a positive reflection. For many, it was mixed and confusing. And for others, it was an overwhelmingly negative picture.

As children, we rarely could choose our mirrors (relationships), and we tended to accept the reflection that we saw as fact. As adults, we can choose our relationships, and we can test the accuracy of our interpretations.

An interesting thing about healthy and motivated people—they are more likely to be casually encouraging about areas others want to grow in. They tend to make a habit of intentionally pointing out areas of strength or possibility they see in others. They are better-quality mirrors. They are more likely to reflect back potential rather than flaws. If you aren't surrounded by quality mirrors—change them.

And remember, you are a mirror for others. Pay attention to what you reflect back to them.

Exercise 2: Track Your "Wins"

A necessary part of a healthy self-image for any effective leader is the belief that you can decide, act, and make an impact. There are different, related concepts for this: agency, internal locus of control, and self-efficacy among them.

Effective leaders lead themselves first. They believe that they can act and create impact. Ineffective leaders tend to believe that they are controlled by external events. Their choices are limited or determined. They are often reactive.

A simple way to cultivate the mindset of an effective leader is with an exercise I first learned from Dan Sullivan. A business coach, author, and speaker, Sullivan describes a practice of defining daily wins.[20]

It works like this: Every day identify at least one "win" that you intend to accomplish that day. Many people find it helpful to write it down in a journal. At the most, choose two wins—one personal and one professional. At the end of each day, write down what your win or wins were for the day.

Now, some days go sideways, and we don't accomplish anything we set out to do. For leaders, this should be a rare experience. But it happens. Even on these days, reflect back and identify something you did well during the day. Perhaps you missed your goals but were still able to be present enough to ask your spouse how their day went and really listened to the answer. Or maybe at some point in the day you withheld an angry response that you really wanted to let loose.

If you are recording two wins a day, over the course of a week, you'll have developed an inventory of 14 wins. Over the course of a month, at least 60 wins. Over the course of a year, more than 700 wins.

The more you pursue this practice, you'll notice three things begin to happen:

1. You'll start to persuade yourself that your choices, decisions, and actions matter. You are a person of impact.
2. You'll start to see even more opportunities for wins throughout your day. Because of the constant practice of setting intent for a win and reflecting back on wins, you'll start to quickly recognize opportunities.
3. You'll start to believe in the promises you make to yourself. People who commit to going to the gym or planning out their day before they start but *don't* do it teach themselves to believe that they break promises. They don't follow through. That is a crippling self-image.

On the other hand, if you consistently follow through, you teach yourself to believe that you will do what you say. That is a confident self-image.

Putting It into Practice: Exercises
- Are there any "mirrors" you need to change? If so, describe the change you need to make.
- What is the first step you need to take to make that change?
- When will you take that step?
- For 21 days, track your "wins."

How I See Others: Leadership Is All About Relationships

As happens in the hallowed halls of Harvard, two sets of students were given two different groups of rats to run through a maze. Dr. Robert Rosenthal, who was conducting the experiment, informed the students that one set of rats was "bright"—smart and good at running mazes. The other set of rats was "dull"—slow and easily confused in a maze.

He asked the students to run their rats and score their times. As expected, the bright rats performed brilliantly and quickly made it to the end of the maze. The dull rats struggled in the same maze. Uncertain, lost, or confused, they just had a more difficult time navigating it quickly. Or so the students thought.

There were, in fact, no bright rats or dull rats. All of the rats were normal lab rats. Dr. Rosenthal had randomly assigned each rat to a group labeled "bright" or "dull." Subconsciously, this difference in expectations led the students to relate to the rats differently. The normal lab rats performed up or down to the students' expectations.[21]

Variations of this study have been repeated many times. It is so widely observed that it has developed names: the expectancy effect, the Rosenthal effect, or the Pygmalion effect.[22] For our purposes let's call it the expectancy effect. Some of the most frequent studies of the expectancy effect focus on the classroom.

A typical study looks like this: Teachers are introduced to students at the beginning of the year. The students are previously unknown to the teachers but have been randomly labeled in some way. In some studies, they are identified as high or low performing. In other studies, teachers are told that the students have been tested and are "expected" or "not expected" to "bloom" this year. Time and again, students live up (or down) to the unspoken expectations.[23]

The expectancy effect is so powerful that a research methodology called "double-blind" trials is now considered a gold standard for some kinds of research, especially medical research. For example, in a double-blind trial for medical treatment, neither the subjects of the research nor the researchers know who has been given the actual treatment or who has received the placebo.[24]

Placebos themselves illustrate another expectation-based effect. A placebo is anything that appears to be a real medication but is instead an essentially neutral substance—for example, a pill made of sugar or an injection of saline solution.[25]

It's well known that people who believe they've been given a medication but instead have been given a placebo can experience the same benefits or side effects that would be expected from the medication. This is called the placebo effect. The purpose of double-blind studies is to control for the placebo effect among the research subjects as well as researcher bias, including the expectancy effect. Both the placebo effect and the expectancy effect describe quantifiable, tangible results that are entirely due to perception. Perception (what is believed) influences reality (what can be observed and measured).[26]

Say what you want about faith and science, but the highest quality science takes faith seriously.

As a leader, how I see others and the expectations I have for them create or inhibit the conditions for their success. A leader's belief about others isn't a dictate, but its power and influence should be recognized.

If how rats are perceived affects their performance, how is this dynamic true in your relationships at work? What about at home or around people in your community?

LEADERSHIP IS A RELATIONSHIP

Leadership is a relationship—this is true always. The way we choose to relate to those around us and the way we help them relate to others are what makes or breaks leaders. This extends to our customers or clients, our employees, our partners, and so on.

We predispose ourselves for or against successful relationships based on how we see others. Since leadership is a relationship, our success as leaders is tied to how we see others.

PUTTING IT INTO PRACTICE: EXERCISES

Try this thought experiment: Identify one person at work (or at home) who makes you feel frustrated or disappointed. Without self-editing, list the first eight words that come to mind that describe this person. How does that list lean? Positive? Negative?

For many people, the list will lean negative. Try this: Rewrite your list with eight true descriptions about that person that are positive or affirming.

For the next 21 days, before you interact with that person, thoughtfully review this new list, imagining that person and those positive traits one by one. Each day add to your list one new positive description—or something you are grateful for—about that person.

Try this and see if your relationship doesn't start to change. It's not a magic wand, but you are changing the conditions for success.

CHAPTER 5

How I See Life: The Key to Unleashing Opportunities

In the 1920s, Viktor Frankl was a medical student in Vienna, Austria. At that time, the student population in Vienna was struggling with a high suicide rate. Frankl organized youth counseling centers to attempt to intervene.

He noticed a relationship between an increase in the number of suicides and the timing of when students received their report cards. Frankl then created a program that focused on counseling students regarding their perspective on their report cards and their grades in general. This resulted in a decline in suicide rates. In 1931, there was a year with no student suicides at all.[27]

Frankl's early endeavors, though lesser known, laid the foundation for his insights on the human spirit, which were further tested during World War II when, being Jewish, he was sent to a concentration camp. There, Frankl observed that a positive attitude significantly influenced the chances of survival amid the atrocities. He noted that individuals who sought meaning and value in their dire circumstances were not only more likely to survive but also maintained better health.[28]

ATTITUDE APPLIES TO LEADERSHIP

In 2008, the developed economies of the world slipped into the Great Recession.[29] I was still fairly new in my practice as a consultant. It was an unsettling time, and two media trends emerged: mainstream media and public radio concentrated on the hardships. Business-centric outlets highlighted entrepreneurial triumphs. I noticed that it was discouraging to read or to listen to the former. But consuming the latter—with their tales of resilience—kindled creativity and optimism.

This was even more evident during the COVID-19 pandemic. Businesses led by optimistic leaders who sought opportunities often thrived and expanded. Leaders who primarily saw threats and risks maintained a "hunker down" state of mind. They withdrew from the market. They made adjustments toward doing less, not toward finding ways to do more.

During 2020 many businesses were hurt or even forced to close permanently. At the same time, all but one of my clients had their best year ever. One key difference was that we maintained a positive, opportunity-focused perspective. The positive perspective didn't magically make things happen. But it allowed those leaders to act in ways that produced valuable results.

WHAT INFLUENCES YOU?

It is important to evaluate our perspectives and what influences them. High-performing leaders actively cut out negative influences. These are influences that don't nourish and may even hold us back. That's a part of our leadership detox. Then, we need to carefully curate the influences we expose ourselves to. This is part of our leadership nutrition.

Here are three ideas that will help you maintain the kind of attitude that generates success:

- Learn to recognize your feelings.
- Practice gratitude.
- Curate media consumption.

RECOGNIZING FEELINGS

When you first wake up in the morning, take a moment to reflect: "What emotion am I experiencing right now?" We all wake up carrying an emotion. For example, last night I didn't sleep well. I woke up feeling disappointed that I needed to get up.

There isn't a right or wrong set of emotions to wake up with. But, if I'm not paying attention, it can be easy to react to that emotion, that sense of disappointment, and carry it into the day. This puts me at greater risk of bringing disappointment into my interactions with others. It may influence the way I foresee how the week will go.

Many leaders launch into the day in reactive mode. But reactivity isn't leadership. It allows other circumstances to lead us. Self-leadership is critical for leaders. This means cultivating self-awareness and intentionality.

So, when we wake up it's worth taking a few moments to identify what we are feeling. Then ask ourselves a few questions:

- Is there any truth to this feeling?
- Is there something here that needs to be addressed?
- What emotion do I want to define my day?

Part of the intent of this exercise is to develop an awareness of how we start the day and to redirect it if needed. But it is also to help us learn to recognize how we show up in any context. Our emotions—whether we're aware of them or not—affect how we see people, events, and our environment.

With some of the people I coach, I've shared a Zig Ziglar story. An author and motivational speaker, Ziglar has talked about waking up, sitting on the edge of his bed, and then clapping his hands and saying, "It's going to be a great day! It's going to be a great day!"[30]

Whenever I tell people about that, they start laughing. It seems ridiculous and silly. However, here's what happens: Many of those people try it. They wake up in the morning, they start clapping their hands, and they start smiling. It's goofy. It's also acting with intent. If there's a spouse or a partner in the room, that person will start smiling and ask what they're doing. It has the effect of positively shifting the start of the day.

By doing this you are deciding, "I am in charge of my attitude for today. I'm willing to be a little ridiculous for about four seconds to accomplish that."

There is nothing magical about this. I don't care if you clap or not. (I don't.) This is about acting with intent: choosing what you want the day to be like and then taking action to move in that direction.

EXPRESS GRATITUDE

Gratitude is one of the most powerful habits and mindsets you can adopt.

Gratitude assumes two things:

1. There is something good in the world.
2. Someone or something else made that good thing possible.

Practicing gratitude helps us see good. It also helps us recognize who or what made that good possible. It cultivates humility.

Arrogant people often feel entitled—not grateful. Gratitude recognizes that some things are just received—not demanded or earned.

As a practice, simply identify three things that you are grateful for each day. Some people like to journal these. Others incorporate this into prayer. Find what works for you. If you want to take this a step further, you can communicate this gratitude to others.

This is such a powerful exercise. I've found that when I'm "stuck" in a negative emotion, gratitude gets me out of it. I'll take the time to identify 10 things that I'm grateful for that relate to the issue I'm struggling with. This isn't always easy, but by the time I've gotten to the 10th "gratitude" my attitude has shifted.

CURATE YOUR MEDIA CONSUMPTION

I mentioned media consumption previously. I bring it up again to reinforce that this cannot be ignored. What we listen to, read, and watch affects how we think and see. In a world with an overabundance of media to consume, those media sources are desperately competing for your attention. Many use anger or fear to help capture and hold your attention.

It's no accident that many of the highest-performing leaders in the world tend to be highly disciplined about what they expose themselves to.

PUTTING IT INTO PRACTICE: EXERCISES

- Pick at least one of the practices above (recognizing feelings, expressing gratitude, or curating your media consumption):
    - What step do you need to take to make this a practice for the next 21 days?
    - What might prevent you from following through?
    - How will you address this so that you do follow through?
    - What support do you need?

CONDITIONING: BUILDING YOUR FOUNDATION

Over-sentimentality, over-softness, in fact washiness and mushiness are the great dangers of this age and of this people. Unless we keep the barbarian virtues, gaining the civilized ones will be of little avail. — Theodore Roosevelt[31]

Introduction to Conditioning

In fitness, conditioning is training that creates a basic, generalized level of fitness.[32] It tends to focus on stamina and physical resilience. For the average person interested in improving their health or losing a few pounds, conditioning may meet all of their goals. In fact, the vast majority of training programs are focused on basic conditioning.

For athletes or professionals in jobs that have high physical demands (military, EMS, police, etc.), conditioning is the foundation that allows them to pursue longer training sessions and higher-level skills and to avoid injury.

Conditioning is often assumed to be mainly about cardio and calories. But there is more to it. Exposing your body to stressors triggers a toughening process that prepares your body to withstand stress without injury. Additionally, your nervous system adapts and grows to support new demands placed on it.

The biggest challenge of conditioning is often the mental aspect. For most people, just showing up to train is the first (very real) victory. Coming back is the second. Making a habit or lifestyle out of fitness is the third. It's only when someone builds the ability and discipline to keep showing up that it becomes possible to learn to push through internal barriers and into new levels of skill or ability.

For leaders, there are strong parallels. There are basic success habits that help your life work better. By adopting these habits, they help you accomplish more—faster and with less effort. For many people, just incorporating these practices into their lives will take them as far as they ever wanted to go. But for leaders, these create the platform that allows them to carry increased responsibility (and stressors) without "injury." Additionally, it allows advanced leadership skills to be practiced and mastered at a sustained level.

When it comes to leadership conditioning, these four areas should be addressed:

- Master your priorities. Set good goals and managing time.
- Follow through. Finish what you started.
- Find and focus intensity. Work hard enough to produce change.
- Practice patience. Learn to delay gratification.

These four lessons, on their own, are worth the price of admission. Applying them as habits in your life will produce lasting benefits.

CHAPTER 7

Priority Management: Become a Master of Space and Time

"I want to stop chasing fires," Andy said. He looked frazzled. "All I do, all day long, is chase after my tail. I never get to work on what I really want to work on."

By most people's measure, Andy is successful. But to him, success feels like driving a rocket-powered car with a three-inch steering wheel on an icy road.

He's not feeling the success. He can't relax. He's afraid of losing control.

There is one simple reason why: he isn't the master of space and time—or at least *his* space and *his* time.

Athletes improve their performance through focused training. World-class athletes dedicate themselves to their sport. They bend their schedules, their eating and sleeping habits, and their training to the demands of their sport. Talent and physical abilities are real, and they matter, but dedication and focus matter more—especially over time.

This is true for leaders as well. Natural talents, training, and experience matter. But unfocused or easily distracted leaders struggle to produce their desired results, let alone maintain them.

TIME MANAGEMENT IS PRIORITY MANAGEMENT

People, especially leaders, do what is important to them. This increases proportionately with the amount of control someone has over their decisions and actions.

There are four critical challenges to this:

- We haven't really decided what is important to us.
- We haven't predetermined how to address competing priorities.
- We confuse immediacy or urgency with importance.
- We don't value (or accept) the steps or conditions required to get to what is important.

So, while we do what is important to us, many of our actions aren't directed toward what is *ultimately* important to us. For example, improving my health and getting back in shape may be important to me. Perhaps it is one of the most important priorities I have. To pursue this, I decide that the best time to work out is in the morning. I purchase a fitness plan, get the gear, and am ready to go. But the night before, I decide I really want to see how a show I've been watching ends. So, I go to bed late. Plus, because I was stimulated by the light of the TV screen, it takes longer to fall asleep.

In the morning, I feel so tired I don't get up in time to work out. I feel rushed, so I grab a Pop Tart on the way out the door and a caramel Frappuccino (with skim milk, please) on the way to work.

What was my priority?

If improving my health is truly a priority, and I'm committed to it, I'll explore the entire priority chain that is required for me to get up early and get a workout in. I introduced a related concept earlier when discussing habit change.

A successful morning workout may depend on how I choose to spend my time 12 hours earlier: I realize I need to go to sleep earlier. To do that, I may need to turn off screens earlier. To do that, I may want to start the show earlier or skip it altogether.

The questions are "What is my priority?" and "What path will get me there?" Not "How do I manage my time?" We all have the same amount of time. Only a few people are intentional about how they use that time.

HOW TO BUILD PRIORITY MASTERY

Tip #1: Determine What Is Important

Your priorities are determined by two things: your values and your vision. Clarity about your values and vision determines where you need to focus your time and attention—your priorities.

This is why defining organizational values and vision is such a useful exercise. When done correctly, it provides focus for the organization. It creates a decision-making framework:

When sorting through decisions, choose the options that clearly contribute to the vision and are in alignment with corporate values.

Any decision that doesn't advance the vision or isn't in alignment with overall values needs to have a pretty amazing justification. Too many decisions of this nature or even just one—if consequential enough—will ensure that your vision will not be accomplished and your values will not be expressed.

Most leaders can grasp this concept around organizations, but they struggle with applying it personally. To help with this, work through the following exercises:

Values Definition

Think about one or two leaders that you find inspirational. Reflect on their attitudes, their decisions, and their behaviors: what are three to five characteristics that you find most inspirational?

Write those down. As you read them, do you believe that those characteristics reflect your own personal sense of values? If not, change or adapt that list until they do. But keep the list short—aim for three to five core values. You may, and likely do, have additional values. But within everyone's list of values, some are more important than others. It's that core few that we are looking for.

Don't worry about getting the "right" list. Just get more clarity. As you use these values over time, you'll develop a sense of how accurate they are. Feel free to change and amend how you define your values as your awareness sharpens.

After developing your list, write a sentence or two that explains what each value means to you. This will help to make your sense of that value crisper; it will become easier to remember and use.

Vision Definition

You can only lead to what you see. Your ability to lead others and yourself is tied to your sense of vision. I'll discuss leading with vision later. For now, we are focused on your personal vision. Your personal vision is simply your sense of what you are trying to accomplish. This may grow and evolve over time. In fact, it should.

Leaders who have more confidence in their ability to set and attain goals usually find this an easier exercise. Leaders still building that confidence should feel comfortable starting where they are at. Maybe the end of the year is as far as you can envision. That's fine. Your ability to develop a larger, clearer, and more compelling sense of vision will grow as you successfully define, pursue, and accomplish smaller visions.

Choose a vision time frame that makes sense to you. This may be one year. It might be many years out.

Then answer these questions with that time frame in mind:

- Who is most affected by my leadership?
- What problems will I solve?
- What opportunities will I capture or create?
- What value will I create or bring to others?
- What makes this important?
- What will it mean if I don't do this?

From your answers to these questions, write one to three sentences that summarize your vision, the best that you see it, right now.

Here are a few tips to help:

- Don't worry about getting it "right." This isn't a test.
- This is a decision-making exercise, *not* a prophetic exercise. You aren't trying to see the future. You are determining what you'd like your future to be like.
- Don't create a plan, write steps, or put any thought into how you'll accomplish this. (Those are important but not helpful right now.)
- Don't compare your vision to that of others.
- Make your vision as big as you can handle right now. If it starts to scare you a little, you are aiming in the right direction.

In my experience, as leaders pursue their vision they become clearer and more specific. For some, this means the vision grows. For others, it adjusts to a more viable pursuit.

Now your priorities. Here is a simplified version of an exercise my clients use with great success:

- Annual priorities. What are the top three to five accomplishments you need to attain this year to make meaningful progress toward your vision while staying in alignment with your values? Which one is the most important?
- 90-Day priorities. What are the top three to five accomplishments you need to attain to make meaningful progress toward your annual priorities? Which one is the most important?
- 30-Day priorities. Same as above.
- One-week priorities. What *one* thing needs to be accomplished this week that will make the biggest contribution to your 30-day priorities?
- Today's priority. What *one* thing needs to be accomplished today that will make the biggest contribution to the week?

To complete this exercise, I recommend that you block out an hour or two, find someplace comfortable where you'll be undisturbed, and then just let yourself go. The first time you complete it, it might take some effort. But this practice becomes easier and faster over time.

Plan on regularly updating the daily, weekly, and monthly priorities as you go. Use 90-day sessions to check overall progress and make any changes that make sense to the annual vision.

Tip #2: Relentlessly Invest in What Is Important

Savers have money. Spenders don't. Investors grow money. Debtors don't.

It's not complicated.

Effective leaders set aside and invest time for their priorities. Ineffective leaders don't. Here's how to do this.

Over the years, I've noticed a difference between my most and least successful clients. The most successful clients do "the work." The less successful don't. The ones who do the work make everything fit around their priorities. They don't try to fit their priorities around everything else.

Calendar blocking. One of the most powerful tools for this is calendar blocking. Calendar blocking is simply setting appointments with yourself to work on priorities. For example, one of my priorities for this year is to complete this book.

I have three chunks of time each week scheduled for working on the book. I rigorously protect those times. My assistant knows not to schedule over them. There are unending reasons to make exceptions about these times, but if I start making exceptions, the book will never be completed.

I recommend calendar blocking to all clients who struggle with getting it all done. Some resist it for months and make very little progress. Then, magically, they start making rapid progress. When I ask what changed they nearly always say, "Calendar blocking."

Here are a few tips that help with calendar blocking:

- Experiment to find the right length of time for you. For many people, 60- to 90-minute chunks of time seem to work well.
- If something comes up that can't be avoided, don't schedule over the time block, just move it.

Attention blocking. Writing and creating content is a major part of what I do. When I first started doing this, it could easily take 30 to 40 hours to complete an article. This was so time consuming and painful that I only wrote three or four articles a year. Then I started to learn how to become more efficient. Now, I write a weekly article in about 90 minutes.

One of the key things I learned was how to prevent interruptions and stay focused.

Many leaders complain that they keep getting interrupted. The answer is simple—stop it. Close your door, and turn off your phone and notifications. Many phones and computers have Do Not Disturb functions. If you struggle with compulsively checking email, there are apps that can block access for a set amount of time.

Personally, I find that certain kinds of music help me focus. Right now I'm listening to Brain.fm. It helps block out noise around me, and there is something scientific (that I can't explain) about how the music is designed that seems to help focus and hold my attention.

In the two decades that I've been consulting and coaching, I've never had a client who couldn't block an hour or two a week to do focused work. This includes emergency room staff.

Energy blocking. We each have only so much energy for creative work or decision-making every day. Mental energy—just like physical energy—has a limit. It can be exercised and grown, but there is only so much of it. So it needs to be spent carefully.

Generally, I do my best focused work in the morning: I'm still fresh, and the day hasn't developed its own momentum. If you don't already know what your most focused time is, pay attention to the times of the day that you do your best work. I block my time with that in mind.

I know I can "refresh" my mental energy—to an extent—with exercise. So, on the days when I do the majority of my heavy thinking, I also break the day in half by doing Brazilian jiu-jitsu (BJJ) in the middle. Even with the time that it takes to train, travel, shower, etc., I'm more productive on days when I train than I am when I don't.

What time of day is best for your focused work?

What conditions seem to help you have the best energy for this work?

Tip #3: Ruthlessly Eliminate Everything That Isn't Important

Aggressively eliminate distractions and work you don't need to do.

Interruptions. The key here is to be ruthless—even unapologetic—about protecting your focused work time. You probably wouldn't let a meeting with an important client get interrupted. Don't let scheduled focus time with yourself be interrupted.

Unimportant work. Some leaders get sucked into completely irrelevant projects: attending meetings that have no point or don't require their attention; answering phone calls that turn out to be cold callers; spending time on decisions or issues that have little to no impact on their priorities. Don't do this. Every single one of these is a bad decision.

Work someone else can do. One of the biggest challenges for leaders is getting entangled in work that someone else can do. Imagine if a skilled surgeon also insisted on taking blood pressure, scheduling patients, billing, and doing maintenance. That surgeon will serve fewer patients, generate less revenue, and employ fewer people. However, if that surgeon gives away all the work that someone else can do, all of those things change. They can help more people, create more opportunities for other professionals, and earn more.

Perhaps it seems humble or an expression of work ethic to do anything you'd ask someone else to do, but you are probably just getting in the way of your success and someone else's opportunity.

PUTTING IT INTO PRACTICE: EXERCISES

- Set aside some dedicated time to work through the tips above.
  - What is your one most important priority for the year?
    - To achieve that, what does your priority for the quarter need to be?
    - The coming month?
    - The coming week?
    - Today?
    - Make a regular practice of reviewing and updating your priorities.

Follow-Through: The First Great Definer of Success

Every January, most gyms experience a temporary bump in attendance. New Year's resolutions, gift gym passes, and new gym gear draw people in. But by April, attendance is back to normal levels.[33] A few of the new people might "stick." Most don't.

Follow-through is the difference. The ability to be consistent over time, follow-through is the primary differentiator between these groups:

- Gym members who are fit and those who aren't
- Leaders who consistently accomplish goals and those who don't

There are many reasons to quit. Some are very understandable. But it doesn't change this basic fact: success is often more about *not quitting* than anything else.

Many people we see as successful aren't the smartest, most gifted, or more privileged. They are simply the ones who kept showing up and doing the work.

WHY LEADERS QUIT

When leaders stop following through, they rarely quit their jobs. Instead, they quit on goals, or they quit on behaviors or habits that eventually produce success. For example, they quit pursuing hard conversations or using good planning or accountability practices. They quit an initiative because it doesn't yield results immediately. They are easily distracted.

There are four primary reasons behind why leaders stop following through:

1. Fixed Mindset

Carol Dweck is a researcher and author who has taught at Harvard, Stanford, and Columbia. She was interested in the characteristics most associated with student success. Her initial research found that this was strongly associated with whether or not a student had a *fixed* or a *growth* mindset.[34] Her observations have been found to be generalizable outside the classroom and apply to leaders.

A fixed mindset is evident when a leader (or anyone else) encounters something that is hard to do, feels unnatural, doesn't produce quick results, or results in initial failure. Leaders with a fixed mindset are more likely to conclude, "I'm not good at this and therefore can't succeed."

They presume that their success is dependent on an innate ability or external social circumstances. If success doesn't come easily, they conclude that success isn't possible. They may conclude that they just aren't wired that way or that they come from the wrong family or that there are unsurmountable social barriers.

In contrast, a leader with a *growth mindset* accepts that success is most often the result of effort. They accept that neither growth nor positive change is likely to just happen naturally on their own. They recognize that the pursuit of goals may include initial periods of discomfort, delay, or even setbacks before results emerge. Leaders with a *growth* mindset accept this for themselves and others.

It's not that natural talent, family background, or social dynamics don't matter. They do. But a fixed mindset is a deterministic perspective that isn't convinced that limits or barriers can be overcome. A growth mindset assumes that overcoming is possible with the right effort.

Leaders must be able to engage challenges and accept that some growth takes effort.

2. Firefighting Syndrome

Leaders often feel unable to pursue goals or dreams (or even take a break) because they are busy putting out fires.

Fires are real. When they occur, they need to be put out. But when organizational fires are a pattern, it's a leadership issue. Either the leader isn't building a culture and structures that will prevent fires, they are allowing someone else to start fires, or they are starting fires themselves.

In most cities, firefighters spend more time responding to accidents and medical emergencies than they do fighting fires these days.[35] Modern societies have learned how to prevent most structural fires, and they don't tolerate arsonists. It shouldn't be any different for leaders.

Leaders who struggle to differentiate between urgent demands and important priorities tend to prefer fighting fires over preventing them. Some leaders prefer it so much they will even start fires.

Fires create a sense of urgency. Urgency has its own energy and creates its own priorities. It simplifies leadership, at least initially, for two reasons:

1. It reduces the need for both decision-making and discipline.
2. Firefighting can allow leaders to swoop in and be the heroes, and they're often recognized as such.

But it isn't heroic to solve a problem they could have prevented. That is often self-service at another's cost. Firefighting leaders *aren't* leading—they are reacting. They are being led by the fire.

3. Shiny-Object Syndrome

Some leaders are easily distracted by new opportunities, ideas, or technologies. They may possess an easily-distractible personality, or they may never have learned to sustain a focused effort or to delay gratification.

Leaders with shiny-object syndrome will often start in productive directions but give up easily. Their attention is diverted when efforts become boring, take too long, or something more exciting shows up.

This is leadership by impulse, which is not actual leadership. Once the impulse or initial enthusiasm for something is gone, so is the attention and effort.

4. Disillusionment and Discomfort

Many leaders start a new initiative with excitement. But after a period of time—days, weeks, or months—when not only are results taking time to show but costs are also adding up, leaders lose their excitement and start to become anxious or frustrated about the pace of things.

This is different from a fixed mindset in that these leaders may recognize that effort is required, but they lose hope that effort or investment will be worth it. Often, their perception of the current discomfort becomes distorted and exaggerated. It becomes easy to believe that the current situation is all that will ever be.

Many leaders fail to lead a team or organization to its potential purely due to believing that the discomfort or cost of change or growth will never end.

Mature leaders will maintain the course even when it doesn't feel good for a time.

THE VALLEY OF DESPAIR

Many of my engagements with clients take six months to a year. A lot can happen in that amount of time. When I first begin with a client, I often draw this picture.

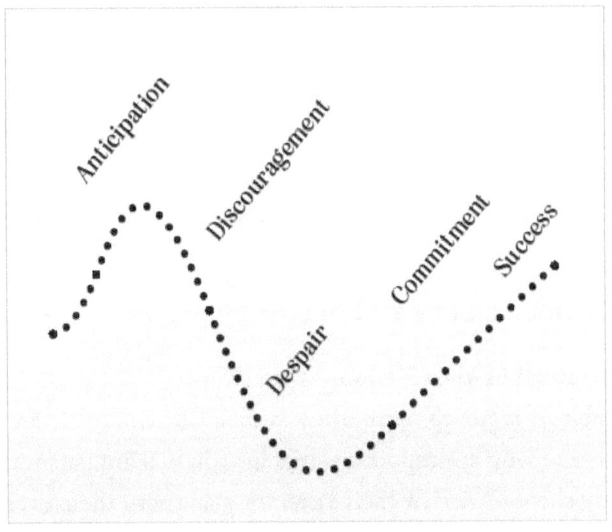

2 The Valley of Despair

I do this to prepare them. But I also do it to protect myself. I've learned that over the course of an engagement, there will almost always come a time where clients get frustrated or want to quit. This happens when they become discouraged or distracted when results take time or they are forced to address issues that are difficult.

Many find fires to distract themselves. Some will be tempted by a quick fix opportunity. Others get impatient that the results didn't arrive the moment they hired me. Still others will decide that the effort isn't worth it and want to quit just before the results come in.

Time issues. People issues. Money issues. Something will come up.

When people talk this way, I know they are in the valley. That's when I remind them of the picture I drew for them. When you feel as if you are in the bottom of the valley, don't stop. Don't wander. The fastest way out of the valley is to climb back up out of it.

This "valley time" may last longer than they want, but it won't last forever. In fact, for my clients, the valley is usually over in a few weeks or months, especially if they keep doing the work. The ability to keep working when going through a valley builds deep resiliency.

Researcher Angela Duckworth calls this "grit."[36] Effective leaders are gritty. Cultivating your ability to follow through is about personal growth. Are you willing to engage in the emotional battle to persevere? Your own desire to quit can be tough enough to wrestle with. What do you do when everyone around you is "done" too?

For most leaders and most teams, follow-through is the answer.

EXPAND YOUR ABILITY TO FOLLOW THROUGH

Remind Yourself of Your Vision—Your Why

Make a habit of regularly reminding yourself of what you are trying to accomplish and why it's important. It helps you reclaim perspective. With many of my clients, I review their vision or goals with them every time we meet. I ask if that vision still matters, if it still excites them.

It's important to be reminded.

On a personal level, I write my vision down. Then I read or recite it to myself each morning. Not only am I reminding myself why I'm doing something that may feel challenging, but the regular recitation helps to sink it into my subconscious. I start to become more oriented toward my goals than I am toward the immediate distractions that will inevitably occur. It supports follow-through.

One More Light Pole

I used to run cross-country in high school. While I was a decent sprinter, cross-country was a challenge for me. Runs measured in yards made more sense to me than runs measured in miles, but many of our training runs were for five miles or more.

Thinking about five miles was too much for me mentally. So, I would pick out a light pole along the trail and commit to reaching it. Then I would reconsider my life choices.

Once I made it to the pole, it would turn out that I hadn't died. I'd look into the distance and find the next pole and just try to make it to that one. By stringing together enough of these short-range goals, I'd eventually complete the run (and then have to bike home).

What is your next light pole? Are you willing to commit to the work it takes to get there?

Surround Yourself with "Gritty" People

It's easier to push yourself when surrounded by others who push themselves. I referred to this earlier: we tend to believe, think, and act like the people we are around.

Surround yourself with people who are great at following through. Avoid people who don't take action or complete their goals. Ideally, find people who are successfully facing situations similar to or just ahead of yours. If these people aren't in your social circle, search for them elsewhere. This is why many high achievers join peer-mentoring groups (masterminds, round tables, etc.). They'll travel to find "gritty" people.

Aggressive Accountability

The highest-performing leaders have or create clear accountability. Leaders who isolate themselves from this end up either underperforming or making costly, avoidable mistakes.

It's no accident that in the consulting and coaching space, the highest-performing consultants and coaches also practice accountability. I've found that to be a rule. They place themselves in peer communities or hire their own coaches not only for the relationships but also for the accountability.

Accountability is often a challenge for leaders—especially owners and high-level executives—because there may be very little or nearly no natural, external accountability. They can't rely on someone else providing it. They have to create it themselves.

I always have at least one coach and a peer community I'm engaged with. Currently, I'm working with two professional coaches on two different topics. It's a significant investment, but it's what produces results.

Find someone to make yourself accountable to. Craig Ballantyne is a *Wall Street Journal* best-selling author and owner of Early to Rise.[37] He's coached and mentored me for years. For accountability, Craig recommends choosing someone you admire and don't want to disappoint. He also recommends making yourself publicly accountable—this could be to your employees, customers, or audience.

When I decided to write my first book, *Conflict and Leadership,* it felt like too big a task. I knew I'd want to quit. So, I announced it to all of my readers. I made myself accountable through my articles and my blog. I don't know if they would have been disappointed if I didn't write it, but I did suspect I would lose credibility if I didn't follow through. That choice motivated me through the long slog of authoring a book.

You *can* learn to follow through. You *can* grow in your ability to stick with it. The question is *will you?*

PUTTING IT INTO PRACTICE: EXERCISES

- Write out your vision and your why. Make a habit of reading it to yourself for 21 days.
- Make yourself get to the next "light pole." Pick a project or task that seems intimidating. Break it down into smaller steps, or light poles. Get there.
- Identify two or three people whom you see as gritty. Find ways to spend more—and ideally regular—time with them. They might be peers or mentors or coaches. If nothing else, pick a podcast with a gritty host. Or read a biography about a gritty historical figure.

Make yourself accountable to someone. You can use your light pole or a series of them to structure your accountability. Ask the person if they'd be willing to meet with you and ask you questions about your goals. (A caveat—most people aren't great at providing accountability. They want to be friends, not coaches, which is why it's often better to find or build a relationship where both sides understand that growth is the primary purpose of the relationship. This is why I and all of the best coaches I know tend to hire their own coaches or form other, formal, accountability relationships.)

Intensity: Learning When and How to Dig Deep

Imagine two people:

The first is a classical guitarist on a stage. She begins to play. You are impressed with her technical skill and precision. She closes her eyes and seems lost in the music. So are you. She draws the entire audience in with her. When the song ends, you feel as if you are waking up. You have no idea how long she played, but you never wanted it to end.

Now imagine a world-class powerlifter. He walks up to a barbell loaded with 1,000 pounds. The room is loud with cheers. He's sniffing smelling salts and snorting like a bull. Then he positions in front of the bar. For a moment, he's quiet and focused. Suddenly his body tenses with exertion. He extends his legs, drives his hips forward, and lifts half a ton from the ground.

The two people are doing radically different things, both of which would be impossible for most others. To get there, they both learned to practice with intensity. Not only did they persevere and show up for training after training, but they learned to push themselves hard. They learned to tolerate discomfort. They learned to push themselves up to and beyond their perceived limits.

As they did, they grew in their skills. Over time, they took their skills to an extraordinary level. Yes, natural talent and genetics likely factor in, but neither talent nor genetics produces those kinds of results on their own.

These two people learned how to practice with intensity. Intensity is two things:

1. An ability to exert themselves near to or at their limits
2. A profound focus of attention and effort

Intensity is uncomfortable. Our brain and bodies prefer homeostasis. Staying within the comfort zone is easier. It's comfortable.

But growth is triggered with intense focus and exertion.

One of the skills of great musicians, athletes, and leaders (in any profession) is the ability to regularly enter—at will—into a state of intensity.

INTENSITY PRODUCES MORE

When it comes to fitness, intense effort is what best triggers growth. Exertion levels typically need to be at least 80% of capacity.[38] At this level of effort, the central nervous system triggers an adaptive response in the body. Athletes who are focused on building strength or power know that they have to push themselves to that point.

For leaders, intensity is the ability to work with complete concentration and focused effort. The reason many leaders don't see the results they want is because they are unable to work with that kind of intensity.

The Flipside of Intensity

On the other hand, both skilled athletes and ambitious leaders have the tendency to take it too far. They do understand intensity, they may be intense people, but they often don't allow themselves enough rest and recovery. The result can be injury, burnout, or poor decisions.

The ideal, both in fitness and in leadership, is to be able to cycle back and forth between times of great intensity and times of meaningful recovery.

I'll go into the topic of rest and recovery later in the book, but I wanted to acknowledge it here. Intensity is important but becomes destructive if not combined with regenerative downtime.

Effective leadership requires the ability to concentrate your efforts. This means putting significant effort into a single area. It also may mean reducing the number of initiatives you are putting your effort into. Either way, enough effort is given to produce results.

PUT IT INTO PRACTICE

Intensity can be and should be practiced.

The most difficult aspect of this for most people is learning to "turn it on." In most cases, this simply means to focus all of your energy and concentration in one direction.

Turning It On: How to Enter Intensity

To practice this, I recommend identifying one of your most important or valuable goals:

- **Focus with sprints.** Set aside regular, short amounts of time to focus exclusively on one of these valuable activities. Research has been done around making these 25-minute blocks, 50-minute blocks, and 90-minute blocks of time. They all seem to help. I doubt the precise amount of time matters as much as the idea of working in short, concentrated sprints.
- **Block (preschedule) time.** You can begin with just one of these sprints per day, but preschedule it. Put it into your calendar. Plan how you will use it.
- **Create a conducive environment.** Close the door, put head-phones on, listen to music that supports productivity, etc. Figure out what works for you. Create or find the space if you don't

have one.

- **Aggressively defend this time.** Turn off alarms, notifications, and phones, let employees and colleagues know you aren't available, etc.
- **Self-correct.** If you get distracted, don't beat yourself up. Just bring your attention back to the task.

Don't wait until you feel ready to be intense. Make it happen.

PUTTING IT INTO PRACTICE: EXERCISES

Answer these questions:

- Are you able to consistently turn it on when you need to?
- What environments seem to be more conducive for intense focus?
- What is one thing that you might start, stop, or change that will help you create intense focus when you want to?

CHAPTER 10

Patience: Learning When and How to Wait

Patience is rarely discussed in fitness or in leadership, but it should be. Patience is related to follow-through. The primary difference is that follow-through emphasizes continued effort over time. For patience, it is the ability to *wait* over time. Specifically, the ability to delay gratification.

To make a gross generalization, there are two kinds of people: those who can't get started and those who can't stop. It's rare that those who struggle to get started end up becoming athletes or successful leaders. The ability to self-start and restart after setbacks or interruptions matters. The drive is important.

But that drive, if not moderated, can create problems. Patience is a key for this. Arguably, impatience is the cause of many—possibly most—injuries and mistakes for both athletes and leaders.

Impatience in Fitness

When pursuing fitness goals, almost no one can get fit fast enough, learn a new skill quick enough, or heal soon enough.

To a significant degree, fitness, supplement, diet, and even medical industries milk these desires. When doing so, they support distorted expectations of what growth and accomplishment should look like. It actually undermines long-term goals because the short-term promises are either false or unsustainable.

People just starting (or restarting) in fitness often struggle with accepting the time it takes to achieve their goals in a healthy and sustainable way. When they don't quickly see the results they hoped for, it can be easy to quit.

Athletes are notoriously impatient for results. This shows up in many areas. Recovery from injury is probably the most common. The most tried and true method for healing most things is to rest. It is also the most reluctantly used. All athletes know the deep frustration (and sometimes even depression) of having to do light calisthenics or physical therapy while everyone else still gets to play.

Leaders, too, often want tangible results—now—when they don't understand that some things just take time. So they get frustrated and quit (this is where follow through is needed), or they try to shortcut the process, or they just become unreasonable in their expectations.

Impatient leaders will place people in positions they aren't ready for. They don't give relationships with prospects time to mature. They don't want to build an organizational foundation that can sustain growth. They want to act, not plan. They don't understand that a task they thought would take 15 minutes has sent an employee down a 15-hour rabbit hole. They may become short-tempered, critical, and accusatory.

People who don't wait well end up not seeing the sustained results they hope for. Not only that but they may also strain or even break relationships along the way.

The business landscape is littered with companies that have experienced a high-watermark year of financial success that burned everyone out. It damaged—and sometimes even killed—the company. There are a number of dynamics behind why that might be, and impatience is a common one.

Four Areas Where Patience Is Needed

Leaders often overestimate what they can accomplish in a day and underestimate what they can accomplish in a year. There are at least four areas where patience is a key virtue. Without it, we are working against ourselves:

1. **Building credibility.** For new leaders, leaders in new positions, or leaders involved in business development or selling, it takes time for them to prove themselves. Find out what people need to experience before extending trust. Then allow time for trust to grow. The only short cut is consistency on your part: Do what you say you will do. Meet the expectations of your position. Give it time. Credibility is weakened by any attempt to force it or demand it from others.

2. **Patience with yourself.** Many leaders struggle with feeling that they don't have everything it takes to do their job. They are probably accurate. But they can grow and learn. Learn to accept and pursue steady, incremental growth. Learn to set a few—but clear—growth goals each year and steadily work to pursue them.

   The 1% growth model is legitimate. Achieve 1% growth each day. In 70 days you'll be twice as good in that area. (Okay, real life might not follow the math. But the principle is true. Consistent, incremental gains add up.)[39]

3. **Patience with others.** Sometimes we suspect or discover that our staff may not have everything they need to do their jobs. That may be true, but they can still grow. Help them identify a few achievable growth goals for each year. Support them in accomplishing those goals. Make the goals measurable so you can track progress. The discipline of identifying the time it takes to grow and sketching out even a rough plan to get there helps you mentally and emotionally accept waiting for growth.

4. **Waiting for projects or initiatives to bear fruit.** One of my best clients, now a national leader in his field, is an energetic, early-adopter personality. He sees and grabs onto new ideas and tools easily and quickly. Unfortunately, when I first started working with him, he was overwhelming his team with all the new ideas, tools, systems, and strategies. It stalled them out as a company. We worked to focus on critical initiatives, and I helped him slow down and wait for new ideas to be fully implemented and then bear fruit. Having accomplished this, they began to achieve and maintain annual growth of no less than 50% with very little turnover.

Gain a reasonable sense of how long it should take a project to show its value, and give it time.

PUTTING IT INTO PRACTICE: EXERCISES

- Which of the four areas above to you think you need to work on the most?
- What are one or two behaviors you can begin to start, stop, or change that will help in that area? How will you make those changes?
- What challenges might you face in trying to develop a new habit?
- How will you address those challenges?
- What support might you need?

STRENGTH: MAKING THINGS HAPPEN

Nothing is so strong as gentleness,
nothing so gentle as real strength. — Saint Francis de Sales[40]

CHAPTER 11

Introduction to Strength

Strength is the ability to make something happen.

A technical definition of physical strength is the ability to generate the force to move (or prevent the movement of) an object. The more resistance an object provides, the more force is needed to move it. The more force an athlete can generate, the stronger that athlete is considered to be.

Strength is the foundation of athletics. All athletics revolve around someone's ability to move either their body or an object or both. Without strength, an athlete cannot be powerful. Without strength, an athlete will only be able to endure a state of weakness.

All leadership revolves around someone's ability to move or influence people and events toward an intended direction. The more (people or events) a leader can move or influence, the better they are at exercising their leadership strengths.

Strength is the basis. Later in the book, we'll look at the concepts of *power* and *endurance*. Without strength, a leader may be able to respond quickly to acute circumstances, but they will be limited in their ability to create movement among others. Without strength, they may be able to hang on for the long haul but will have little impact or influence.

The previous topics on nutrition, environment, and conditioning are critical to being able to develop and grow in leadership strengths. In many ways, the previous topics can be summarized as managing or leading yourself. The best leaders do this well.

For emerging leaders, the ability to lead and manage themselves often comes *before* being presented with leadership opportunities. For experienced leaders, going back to these basics is often what unlocks the next level of opportunity or results. But neither nutrition nor conditioning alone will create an athlete. Similarly, practicing the principles behind leadership—nutrition, environment, and conditioning—aren't enough to provide actual leadership. Instead, they create the conditions within which effective leadership can grow.

James Kouzes and Barry Posner are researchers out of Santa Clara University. They studied thousands of leaders from around the world and in diverse industries. The organizing question of their research was "What are these leaders doing when they are at their best?"[41]

Their book *The Leadership Challenge* emerged out of this work. In it, they identify what they call the "five practices of exemplary leadership":

- Model the way
- Inspire a shared vision
- Challenge the process
- Enable others to act
- Encourage the heart [42]

These five practices equate to the five core strengths of effective leaders. As an individual grows in these five strengths, three things happen:

- They become more effective as a leader.
- They begin to be *recognized* as a leader.
- They build their *credibility* and *influence*.

These five practices provide a map for new leaders to help them know where to focus.

Most successful and experienced leaders have developed some of these strengths, but they will nearly always have a weak spot as well. If you've ever felt limited or held back in some way in your leadership potential, the chances are high that your area of weakness is responsible.

The previous chapters covered the foundation principles. It's difficult to lead well, for long, without having those principles in place. But to really begin to do the work of leadership, you need to build these five leadership strengths.

Modeling the Way: Become Someone Others Can Follow

I received a call from a Fortune 500 company. "We have a problem within our organization, a behavioral one. I was wondering if you could help us turn it around?"

As I explored this with the caller, I discovered that she was looking for someone who could lead staff workshops across their organization. Given that they have over 30,000 employees, that is a lot of workshops.

This would be a bonanza for a consulting firm: a huge, labor-intensive project that wouldn't require a lot of skill. We could hire an army of trainers, give them a script, and let them go at it.

I asked, "Is this behavior prevalent on the executive team?"

"Yes," she answered.

"Is it also prevalent on the board?"

"Yes," she answered.

"Then they are who I need to work with. They've set the tone and culture for the entire organization. Everyone else is just reflecting them. If they change their behavior, it'll be simple to make downstream changes."

"Oh, they wouldn't go for that."

"Then the problem won't change. It doesn't matter how many trainings people are forced to go through."

Leadership behavior is reflected throughout the organization— leaders need to demonstrate the behaviors they desire from others.

BELIEFS > VALUES > GOALS AND PRIORITIES > BEHAVIOR

The head instructor at the Brazilian jiu-jitsu (BJJ) gym where I train often wraps athletic tape around his big toes. I was curious why and asked. He told me that his skin tended to crack under his toes. He taped them to protect the skin. Then he said something interesting: "Once I started taping my toes, I notice everyone else started taping their toes too."

People mimic leaders.

The science behind this is interesting. We all have mirror neurons in our brain. These mirror neurons influence us to mimic the behaviors of those we observe.[43] This can sound kind of woo-woo, but it's not. I taught a class on this topic for our local chamber of commerce. I split the audience of business leaders into groups of three or four and gave them a discussion topic.

Then I went around the room and photographed the groups. In each group you could see that the participants tended to all sit the same way. If the speaker, or whoever seemed to have the most dominant personality, was sitting forward, elbows on knees, the others tended to as well. If that person was leaning back, with their ankle crossed over their knee, the others followed suit.

As we debriefed their assignment, I talked about the power of mirroring. I stressed the importance of a leader's awareness of this dynamic, especially because we often aren't aware of our behaviors, so we aren't aware of what people are mimicking.

The concept was novel. The participants were interested but not persuaded, so I showed them the pictures I had just taken.

They were shocked. Everyone wanted to see the photo with them in it. And in spite of seeing themselves as independent-minded, strong leaders, most saw that they had unconsciously mimicked those they sat with.

Now they believed me. Mirroring isn't just a clever leadership philosophy—it's a powerful part of our neurological hard wiring. The more influential or powerful someone is perceived to be, the more likely it is that others will take their cues from them.

So, we tape our toes without realizing why. Or we cross our ankles when talking to someone. Or we mimic more important behaviors related to performance: quality, timeliness, honesty, respect, communication patterns, approaches to conflict, and so on.

How we act as leaders, consciously or otherwise, is observed and mirrored by others.

Behavior

How we act reflects our values and beliefs.

This is especially true when no one is looking, when it's easy to rationalize or hide a poor decision or when we are tired, rushed, angry, or stressed.

Behavior is rooted in our beliefs and values. We act out of what we truly believe.

Of course, some behavior can be enforced through external means such as punishments or rewards for acting a certain way. But that requires constant energy and effort on the part of leadership to monitor and enforce the desired behaviors.

Leaders usually have fewer external constraints. As a result, how they actually behave tends to be a fairly accurate reflection of their internal values and beliefs.

People watch leaders closely. Leaders (even the nicest of ones) have power and influence. People are aware of this and often try to interpret what that leader wants, expects, and values.

What Leaders Model

Leaders primarily model three things through their behavior: what they align themselves to, their attitudes, and their expectations about performance.

Alignment. Leaders demonstrate the degree to which their actions and choices are in alignment with stated goals, vision, and values. This is a demonstration of character.

When people observe that leaders act in alignment with stated values and vision, it nurtures a broad range of credibility. The leader is viewed as more credible because they are doing what they say people in the organization will do. The leader's behavior reinforces the credibility of the value and vision and the organization as a whole.

Attitudes. Attitudes are catchy. Leaders who are positive, encouraging, and upbeat are more likely to find that their staff is as well. Leaders who are hard workers, who are not afraid to get their hands dirty or of using a little elbow grease, will also discover that their team tends to work hard as well.

Conversely, leaders who are comfortable gossiping or engaging in us/them behaviors will find factions developing. Leaders who denigrate others or take a loose attitude toward safety or ethics will find that others will as well.

Performance. Some people have a built-in quality gauge. They will always give you their best effort. But many others are looking for cues to understand: "How good is good enough?"

Many leaders unintentionally send cues about performance. For example, a leader might cut corners to get a project out on deadline. That leader may be focused on getting a project delivered on time, but the louder message about performance or quality is often what is heard.

That same leader may believe they value quality. Very few leaders would say otherwise, but because of poor time or project management, quality may be sacrificed to avoid being late.

In these instances, employees tend to pick up on both the willingness to sacrifice quality as well as the poor time and project management behaviors that drove it. It becomes a negative feedback loop.

Why Matters Less Than *What*

Why we do things matters, but *what* we do is what people see. That often matters more.

In college, I led a student organization that primarily operated through smaller groups. One of my primary roles was to identify, mentor, and support new leaders. I also led one of the small groups directly.

In the group I led, I put in the time and effort to prepare. My preparation allowed me to relate in a very casual and relaxed way. I could embrace changes and hiccups in the group's agenda without it being evident that they were at risk of going off course. One result of this was that the group meetings went well and were popular.

One new leader I was mentoring was struggling with his group. I attended one of his meetings and watched his behavior. I could see that he was doing and saying many of the things that I did and said. Especially, he adopted my casual and relaxed way of leading the group. But he hadn't done the preparation I had done. He wasn't clear on the outcomes he wanted to accomplish and how to get there, so his meetings wandered. When something unexpected occurred, he wasn't prepared for it.

He was mimicking me, but he had seen only part of the picture. I had modeled casual, relaxed behavior, but I hadn't demonstrated what I did beforehand that allowed my apparently casual approach to work.

Our intent in modeling matters. But what people actually pick up on matters more. Leaders should watch for common traits or behaviors among our teams or people. Expect that our observable sense of alignment, our attitude, and our behaviors will be mirrored by them.

At the time, I didn't know how to model something that felt invisible, but if my past self could listen to my current self, here are some ideas I'd implement:

- Organize group prep times where all of the leaders would prepare together
- Create a preparation template for all group leaders and refer to it regularly
- Consistently make references to how I prepare in my normal communication with group leaders

It would take experimentation. I don't know what answer would work the best—perhaps a combination or perhaps something completely different. But I do know that being intentional about modeling will help others see what I intend them to see. When that happens, they are likely to model it.

POSITIVE BEHAVIORS

When you see others modeling positive traits, reflect on the specific behaviors that you are demonstrating. You want to identify those so that you can repeat them. Also, you can begin to highlight or teach these behaviors to your management team. This is part of how you intentionally architect your culture.

Highly successful leaders often have ways of relating that feel so natural they don't think about it. This is their special sauce, so to speak. If we want people to copy our special sauce, we need to be willing to write down and share the recipe. Don't expect others to just figure it out.

NEGATIVE BEHAVIORS

When we see common negative behaviors in our team, we need to be willing to consider how we might be modeling those. For example, if many members on a team avoid practicing or taking accountability, senior leadership usually does so as well.

If our organizations or teams are dealing with problem behaviors, it's worth reflecting on the possibility that we are just seeing ourselves through them. The solution to this is to bring ourselves into alignment and ensure that our behaviors reflect that alignment.

High performers will move to a place that they feel aligned with.

Organizations known for their high standards and quality reflect the values of their leaders. A mismatch between leadership values and organizational standards won't persist. The organization will either reject the leader or the standards of the organization will change.

High performers are attracted to places where there is alignment—not just in words but in the behaviors of leadership. Confident and skilled people who treat others well will look for workplaces where leaders do the same. Conversely, they'll leave workplaces where they don't feel aligned. This is part of what shapes and reinforces organizational cultures.

You lead out of who you are. This is especially true when it comes to modeling the way. Who you are—and especially how you behave—is what others will see, follow, and mimic.

The primary leadership issues that leaders wrestle with *don't* have to do with technical or business knowledge or skills. They have to do with mindsets, character, and emotional maturity. Those are the kinds of things that you can't fake for long.

PUTTING IT INTO PRACTICE: EXERCISES

1. Identify one positive behavior. Choose one that contributes to the success of the organization and is widespread among those you lead.
   - Name it and briefly describe it in one sentence.
   - In no more than two or three sentences, describe how you demonstrate this behavior.
   - Explore ways you can introduce this behavior as early as possible into your recruiting and onboarding processes. It will function as a magnet and a filter in recruiting. It will help new hires understand how to quickly align.

2. Identify a positive behavior that you believe you practice but *isn't* demonstrated among your team (for example, my college habit of preparation).
   - Name it and briefly describe it in one sentence.
   - In no more than two or three sentences, describe how you currently demonstrate this behavior.
   - Decide on one or two options for how you could more openly or transparently demonstrate this behavior to others.
   - Make a point of incorporating these new behaviors into your daily leadership.

3. Identify a negative behavior that is demonstrated within your team.

    -   Name it and briefly describe it in one sentence.
    -   Estimate the cost or consequences of this behavior.
    -   In no more than two or three sentences, describe how you might currently model this behavior.
    -   Develop options for how you might change your own behavior. Choose one that you will incorporate into your daily leadership.
    -   Identify what support or help you might need to change your behavior.

Inspire a Shared Vision: How to Motivate Action

When I was young, my family lived on a farm. Among other animals, we raised chickens. At times, you need to move chickens toward the same location, but it's hard to herd chickens. If you try to herd or push them in a direction, they just scatter. But if you give them a common focus, like food, they will flock to you.

Leadership can feel like herding chickens. When it does, you know that those you lead don't have a common focus. They aren't inspired by a shared vision.

You have to create that.

WHAT IS A SHARED VISION, AND WHY DOES IT MATTER?

Of the five leadership strengths or practices, it is the ability to *inspire a shared vision* that most powerfully differentiates a leader from everyone else.

To inspire a shared vision, two components are needed:

1. A compelling picture of the future
2. That picture shared by multiple people

A vision is a mental picture of the future. When that vision is compelling, it will typically motivate movement. The more compelling it is, the more movement it can generate.

When multiple people are able to "see" the same (or a very similar) mental picture, they are more likely and more willing to move together. The more people who see the same vision, the easier it is to lead them toward a similar goal.

When many people clearly see the same vision or goal, and they are inspired to pursue it, much of a leader's work is done, and the remaining work is easier.

Visionary Leaders?

Richard Branson. Coco Chanel. Elon Musk. Arianna Huffington. Many leaders are visionary in the classic way we understand it. They seem to easily see over the horizon, recognize hidden strengths, and identify undiscovered opportunities. They create complete and compelling ideas of what could be.

But not all leaders are like this. And they don't need to be.

Some leaders are stronger at implementing or administrating organizations. Others are very effective at nurturing and growing people. Some are incredible at pulling together resources. Others are exceptional at overseeing the use of those resources.

It is *not* critical that an individual leader be the original source of vision for an organization. But it *is* critical that all leaders somehow come into the possession of a clear vision, one that they can clearly articulate and one that generates their own passion and drive so they can inspire others.

What Makes a Vision Inspiring?

An *inspiring vision* is one that taps into people's intrinsic motivation. This is usually a desire to gain (or not lose) three things:

- **Security.** Feeling financially, relationally, physically, or otherwise safe, secure, and stable.
- **Significance.** Feeling as if you are a person of value, you bring value to others, and others recognize you for this value. This includes a sense of purpose.
- **Satisfaction.** Feeling peace, contentment, and happiness—usually in the basic things of life.

Whatever the vision is, if people see and believe that getting there helps them increase or protect these core motivations, they'll pursue it. The more they believe this vision will satisfy these core desires, the easier it becomes to motivate them in that direction.

When a group shares a compelling vision, magical things happen:

- **You tap into motivation.** This fuels commitment and performance.
- **Alignment is easier.** This increases productivity and decreases conflict.
- **Management becomes simple.** It is easier for people to self-manage since everyone has a shared sense of what they are trying to accomplish. To an enhanced degree, they can use their own problem-solving abilities, as opposed to waiting to be told what to do.

Great Vision That Is Not Shared

I worked with a partner in a company who had a fantastic vision and great ideas, but they weren't shared by his other partners. He was enormously frustrated by this.

His partners were also frustrated. They felt as if they were being accused of failing in a vision that they never saw or committed to.

His vision was clear. It was needed. But vision alone isn't enough.

His leadership task was the process of learning to *inspire* his partners to develop a *shared* vision. You can't demand this. When that is accepted, both work and life become much easier. More on how to do this later.

Does Vision Need to Be Huge, Hairy, and Audacious?

No, vision doesn't need to be huge, hairy, or audacious. But it does need to be inspiring and compelling. A vision that is merely an anticipation of a future that no one really cares about and will happen without any additional effort is blah. It won't motivate.

That being said, sometimes leaders are encouraged to develop such large visions—untethered from any sort of reality—that they end up just frustrating and demotivating others. A key element of making an inspiring and shared vision is that people need to see (and believe) that they can build it.

It's a balance: big enough to be inspirational but realistic enough to be within reach—or at least getting close.

A compelling vision needs to be able to guide decision-making. It needs to be clear enough that people can actually imagine it. It needs to be so clear that they imagine the same thing.

Only in very rare occasions does a vision need to speak to the outside world. Marketing experts are wrong—how you communicate your vision mostly doesn't matter to anyone on the outside. There are a few very discrete situations where communicating your vision to outsiders matters, such as fundraising for a start-up or a nonprofit, because sometimes all you have is vision. But even then, while the vision needs to be clear, the plan should be clearer.

Aside from that, frankly, very few people care what your vision is. They want to know what you will do for them or the things they care about. Don't let the marketing tail wag the dog.

But *inside* the organization, vision matters tremendously. Your people are your primary audience. Don't lose sight of that.

The Challenges of Vision

Naturally visionary leaders are people who easily develop ideas of what could be. They can become frustrated when it's difficult to gather buy-in or commitment from others. They may find that their vision is met with apathy or even rejection.

Sometimes, their vision *will* generate enthusiasm. But commitment is expressed along these lines: "Great idea! We love it! Let us know how it goes." These leaders struggle to translate *my* vision into *our* vision.

In addition, visionary leaders may struggle with their own commitment. Some visionary leaders have burned their audiences. They pursued a vision that caused harm, or they have a track record of poor execution or follow-through.

Some are susceptible to the shiny-object syndrome. Others just get tired. Some are not willing (or don't understand how) to plan and execute a vision effectively. As a result, their leadership landscape becomes littered with partially completed projects, many of which were good ideas. This undermines credibility.

It doesn't even have to be you who didn't follow through. If the people you lead were previously led by a visionary leader who didn't deliver, they may transfer their past experience onto you. It may not feel fair, but you'll need to build credibility. This is done by consistently doing what you say you will do.

The Struggles of Leaders Who Aren't Naturally Visionary

I often meet leaders who struggle to develop a sense of vision. They may be great problem solvers or implementors, but they don't easily come up with ideas that feel visionary. There are very specific reasons for this. Some are about personality or style of leadership, but most are due to having insufficient self-confidence or not having a sense of self-efficacy or fire in their belly. These are foundational issues that I addressed in the first section of "Healthy Habits: Nutrition and Environment."

I've walked many leaders and even teams through the process of not being visionary to being very visionary just by helping them work on the fundamentals of how they see themselves, others, and life. This is usually accomplished by helping them consistently set and reach goals and by addressing issues in their relationships with others.

Leaders who learn that they can set and achieve goals will often find that their sense of the future has expanded. Their ability to see opportunities sharpens. Their perception of risk changes.

Here's the interesting thing. Many leaders *appear* to be confident. They may dress, talk, and walk confidently. Within a narrow set of controlled or accustomed parameters, they may be confident. But they aren't confident out in the wild, so to speak. And vision is out in the wild. It's blue water sailing where circumstances may not be fully knowable and are rarely controllable.

It's for this reason that it's important for leaders to spend time out in the wild. This simply means pushing their comfort zones. For many leaders, being out in the wild means holding their team accountable and addressing poor behavior. For some, I've recommended such relatively tame and seemingly unrelated experiences such as joining Toastmasters, consistently meeting with a personal trainer, or taking ballroom dance lessons. (All were effective *in the right situation*.)

The point isn't for the leader to master this new skill. The point is to learn that discomfort doesn't equal death. Go ahead. Be uncomfortable. Put yourself in environments you can't control. You'll become a better leader.

There are two basic methods for developing a shared vision. Both have pros and cons, and they tend to work better together. They are *vision casting* and *vision gathering*.

VISION CASTING

Vision casting is what people tend to think of as visionary leadership. Effective vision casting happens when a credible leader has a vision for the future that taps into the shared aspirations of others. It's a great idea that, when communicated, prompts other people to say, "Yes—I want that!"

- **Pros.** It is fast. It's great for emergencies or urgent situations. It can be helpful when the leader or leadership team functionally retains the real power in a situation (for example, the owner of a private company).

- **Cons.** It is often harder to gain commitment from others. Some people are reactively resistant to change or ideas that are unfamiliar. Others tend to say, "Yes—I want that! You go ahead and do that for us!" Due to lack of commitment, vision casting often requires a lot of work to maintain after the vision has been cast. These kinds of visions are often less sustainable in the long-term.

If you are a natural vision caster but find that you struggle at times to get buy-in for your vision, try these things:

1. **Assess and establish credibility.** If you are a new leader, you'll need to build credibility by proving you can follow through on smaller goals. If you've never delivered on something as large or demanding as your current vision, you may need to be patient and demonstrate you can follow through with smaller visions. If you've not followed through in the past, you'll need to rebuild your credibility. If a previous leader didn't follow through, and you've inherited that lack of trust, you'll need to demonstrate that you are different.

    Take the time to build a foundation of trust.

2. **Write out your vision.** Describe it as clearly as you can. Especially try to use language that evokes images in the mind's eye. The use of metaphors or stories can help with this. As an example, at the beginning of this chapter I told a story about herding chickens. That creates a mental image that make it easier for others to connect. Some people find it helpful to create an actual drawing of their vision.

    Articulate your vision in such a way that others easily see it.

3. **Identify your stakeholders.** Stakeholders are people who have an interest in your vision. By "interests," I mean they have needs or desires that may be affected by or could influence the vision.

    In this case, who is the audience for your vision? Whose buy-in do you need or want? Whose interests do you need to pay attention to? Is there anyone who can prevent your vision? Visionary leaders can stumble when they attempt to sell their vision to the wrong audience. Many visionary leaders will prefer to talk to easy or friendly audiences. But these audiences may not be composed of the people who need to be engaged.

    Know whose buy-in you need.

4. **Ask your stakeholders about their interests.** The more your vision appears likely to help someone meet their interests, the more likely they are to support it.

    It's best to ask. This helps us avoid making assumptions or projecting our interests onto others. However, it's difficult to ask people, "What are your interests?" Instead, I find it helpful to ask people about their goals or ambitions, especially as they relate to the subject of your vision. Additionally, you can ask about their concerns, frustrations, or the challenges they see.

    When you know someone's interests, describe how those interests can be met through your vision. If your vision doesn't persuasively address their interests, it will be difficult if not impossible to gain or retain their buy-in. Either you are speaking to the wrong audience, or you need to reconsider your vision. It's possible that your vision was built on faulty or incomplete assumptions. This doesn't mean it was wrong, but it may need to be adjusted to better fit the interests of others.

    You'll get buy-in when your vision is the answer to their interests.

VISION GATHERING

Vision gathering is a process of listening to the shared interests, aspirations, and concerns of others. Then you work with them to develop a picture of the future that meets those shared interests, aspirations, and concerns. It is often the best approach in situations where there is a need for long-term commitment or when a leader has limited power.

- **Pros.** Vision gathering tends to be "sticky." The process creates buy-in and ownership. It doesn't require that any particular leader have the vision—anyone can do it. It's what I do as a consultant. I don't come with a vision for clients, but I often help clients develop and clarify their vision.

- **Cons.** It takes more time up front. It is less predictable or controllable. It requires a high level of skill to be able to guide a group of people through difficult conversation to consensus without creating a flavorless, meaningless vision by committee.

Here are steps that you can use to gather vision with a group:

1. **Clarify shared values.** A colleague of mine, Andrew Hollo, defines values this way: "Values are beliefs that, when shared and visible as behavior, predict your success."

    Value statement exercises are often dumbed down into marketing slogans. It's fine to use values in your marketing. But the reason you define them should be to create coordinates for alignment within your organization.

    When organizational values are well defined, it helps everyone broadly understand what is important and expected.

    Clear values have these two components:
    a. **They are few.** If all values are special, then no values are special. Organizations err when they develop long lists of values. The intent is usually to say, "All these things are important." But in practice, they will not treat all values

as equally important. Some values will be referenced frequently. Others are forgotten. When there is a conflict between two values (for example, timeliness vs. quality), one will win out.

Get out a sharp knife and pare your list down to your top three to five values. Long lists of values become unread platitudes. Short lists can become powerful tools.

b.   **They are defined.** When you say that honesty, quality, or respect is a value, what does that actually mean to you? Not everyone defines those terms the same way. Respect can look very different for different people. I encourage clients to write value narratives. This may be a few descriptive words. It might be a sentence or two. Briefly and succinctly describe what the value means and how the value should be expressed.

2.   **Clarify core interests.** To understand core interests, it often helps to get people talking, especially if they are talking about values or goals or priorities.

As they talk, ask questions like these:

- What is the most important thing we can accomplish [within a specific amount of time]?
- What makes this [value, solution, idea] important to you?
- What do you feel will be lost—or not gained—if we don't pursue this?
- Do you prefer suggestion A or B? What makes that suggestion preferable to you?

Listen for themes—frequently repeated, widely shared, or similarly aligned.

I'll often paraphrase what I hear: "It sounds like this group is very concerned about how to pursue growth without losing the 'family' feel of your culture. Does that sound correct?"

Don't worry about paraphrasing correctly if you give them room to correct you. If you are correct, they'll confirm it. If you misunderstood, they'll correct it. Regardless, you are listening, and they'll feel that.

3. **Determine a timeline.** Most people have imagination horizons. They can imagine just so far out in time and no further. Organizations that have little experience with planning, are unstable, or are in a highly unstable environment often have nearer horizons. They may only be able to imagine a year out. As the organization grows in experience and confidence, becomes more stable, and learns how to manage the stormy seas of its environment, the horizon expands. It becomes easier to imagine many more years out. I've worked with oil companies that had planning horizons that were decades out. They had the planning experience, confidence, and need to think that far out.

    Choose a timeline that matches but challenges where your team is at.

4. **Draft a vision statement.** Once you've identified core values and core interests, you usually have the core ingredients of a vision. I call these "vision components."

    Imagine vision components like ingredients in your cupboard. Let's say you open the cupboard and see chocolate chips, flour, sugar, and vanilla. All we've described are ingredients. But many people will also have a picture (a vision) of cookies or something similar that comes to mind. No one will imagine spaghetti or eggplant parmesan.

    At a minimum, you can say something like this: "Here are our core vision components: we want to pursue growth, we want to maintain a family culture, and we want to be seen as regional leaders in our industry." That's a solid start. It provides direction and clarity. It's enough to begin moving and planning.

Let your team affirm or edit this list. Then tie it to the timeline and work with the team to sharpen it—for example, "Within the next three years, we want to achieve growth [as defined by X and Y]. We want to continue to experience [specific elements] of family culture, and we will be regional leaders in both sales volume and customer satisfaction."

Now you have gathered a great vision and one that is a highly useful tool. It's a slower process to develop it. But along the way, you've created alignment, gathered buy-in, and engaged commitment as well.

Note: It is often difficult for a leader (or any insider) to facilitate these conversations effectively. Consider bringing in a skilled, neutral consultant to help - so that you can fully participate without dominating the discussion.

PUTTING IT INTO PRACTICE: EXERCISES

- Decide whether you want to try vision casting or vision gathering.
- Either way, start small. Identify something simple and noncontroversial to start with. A vision for a small change or improvement is legitimate. The skills to develop a unified vision around an employee recognition policy or reorganizing a shop will carry over to larger issues.
- Walk through the steps described above.
- Afterward, evaluate what you've learned.
- What worked, and what will you do again next time?
- What didn't work as expected? What will you do differently?

CHAPTER 14

Enabling Others to Act: The Key to Building People

For years, I trained an athlete who was a gymnast in high school. As an adult, she was a military officer. She also regularly participated in and completed ultraendurance races. By "ultra," I mean 1,000-plus miles. She looks petite and feminine, but she is tough. On more than one occasion, she has shown me up in terms of raw athleticism and skill.

I started introducing dead lifts into our regular workouts. Suddenly she became dainty. If she could get away with it, she'd lift the bar without any plates on it. I had trained with her for years, and I knew she could easily handle more.

Once I ensured that her form was consistently correct, I loaded the bar with roughly her body weight in iron. She slumped and looked at me.

"I can't lift this!"

The issue wasn't her ability. She had that in spades. It was how she saw herself. We worked on that. My help mostly consisted of saying, "Yes, you can. You cranked out 100 pull-ups last week. You can handle your bodyweight. Start your set."

And she did.

Here's the takeaway: I didn't lift the weight for her. I didn't make it easier. I enabled her to lift the weight for herself.

ENABLING OTHERS TO ACT

There is an inflection point that only some leaders experience. It happens when leaders learn to empower others to act. These leaders discover how to expand the scope and impact of their leadership dramatically.

The best learn how to do so while simultaneously reducing their own workload. And they do this by learning how to focus, nurture, and release the ability of their team.

In contrast, less effective leaders tend to create or reinforce dependency on themselves. They attempt to maximize their ability to operate in isolation. They simply may never have been taught another way. Or their identity or sense of worth may be closely tied to being seen a certain way. Or they just might like working in isolation.

There can be lots of reasons. But they *always* limit out faster. They hit a lower max.

They may feel that they or their team should be performing at a higher level. And they are probably right. But they can't get there without enabling others to act. Leaders need to shift from focusing on maximizing their ability to maximizing the ability of others.

ENABLING OTHERS TO ACT AND SERVANT LEADERSHIP

At the beginning of this book, I introduced the concept of *servant leadership* as an underpinning philosophy. Enabling others to act is at the core of servant leadership. Many leaders misunderstand servant leadership to be something along the lines of being willing to do anything they ask their people to do. There is a place for that, but often, that's just simply getting in other people's way.

Robert Greenleaf, who coined the term "servant leadership," articulated this concept well in his book *Servant Leadership: The Path to*

Legitimate Power and Greatness. "The best test as a leader is: Do those served grow as persons; do they become healthier, wiser, freer, more autonomous, more likely themselves to become leaders?"[44]

And there lies the rub. Many people who genuinely want to be servant leaders also (usually subconsciously) find they like being the person others depend on. It provides a sense of identity, value, and purpose. It appears not just benign but, possibly, saintly.

What Robert Greenleaf suggests—and what Kouzes and Posner later confirmed through research (and I agree with)—is that true servant leadership builds people who need the leader less.

That last statement is why we often don't see true servant leadership. It explains why many well-intended leaders struggle to grow their teams and organizations. They don't understand that growth comes from giving away authority and the ability to act.

Leaders who empower others to act increase their influence. They expand their ability to build and lead larger or more complex projects or organizations. Getting there requires letting go and empowering others.

HOW TO EMPOWER OTHERS TO ACT

There are two primary areas to practice if you want to empower others to act.

1. Create Psychological Safety (a.k.a. Build Trust)

The first is creating psychological safety within the group (even if the group is just yourself and one other person).

Psychological safety is the long way of saying "trust." Kouzes and Posner call this "fostering collaboration by building trust and facilitating relationships."[45] When people trust each other, because they feel as if they can communicate and engage freely with each other, they work together more effectively.

Psychological safety is not built by creating trigger-free zones, removing challenges, or disagreements. It is built by creating a level of mutual trust and respect so that robust conversations and even disagreements can occur and be productive.

The athlete I began the story with felt safe with me. That sense had been built out of years of training together. So, an abrupt answer of "Yes, you can. Do it," was appropriate and helpful. If I was working with someone who didn't know me and who was very self-conscious physically, my response would have adapted to what was needed to help them grow.

This is an important distinction. Here's an example from Brazilian jiu-jitsu. Psychological safety on the mats occurs when you trust your training partners. When you do so, both partners may put 100% into attempting to force each other to tap out. But they trust that each is also looking out for each other's safety. Both know that winning is less important than learning and the relationship.

When that sense of safety is lacking, people tend to avoid training with each other. Or they focus on either domination or survival. This is accepted in a tournament and makes sense in self-defense but not for training or skill development.

The primary way to create psychological safety is to model the behaviors that support it. Even in BJJ, the more senior or experienced partner should work to control the pace and energy of the match. If I'm training with someone who seems aggressive and "spazzy," I'll attempt to use my words and body language to slow down and lower the intensity of the match. I accept that my opponent might not have physical or emotional self-control. So, I will approach the match in a way that keeps us both safe and injury-free.

If I'm training with someone who is the opposite and seems overly cautious and hesitant, I'll attempt to relate in a way where they feel safe to engage. Again, their welfare and experience are my primary concerns—not winning the match.

For leaders, this includes demonstrating appropriate vulnerability, asking for and engaging with the input of others, and acknowledging and owning mistakes.

Appropriate Vulnerability

People know that leaders are human, but many leaders are afraid to have their humanity discovered. So, they attempt to maintain a picture of always being authoritative, well-tempered, and all-knowing. They are unwilling to be seen making mistakes.

Appropriate vulnerability, instead, means willing to be self-effacing. You may not know everything, but you can be curious about things. You will make mistakes, and you will focus on learning from and fixing mistakes quickly—not denying that they can happen. Telling stories about mistakes you've made and lessons you've learned can go a long way toward helping others connect.

Asking for and Engaging with the Input of Others

I often advise my coaching clients to go to their teams and say, "I'm trying to accomplish X. What are one or two specific suggestions you have for doing this?" The leaders aren't asking for their team to provide direction. They are asking for input. I work with them to take all of the input, make sense of it, and then choose a direction informed by that input.

When your team sees you doing this, it tends to raise their sense of your credibility. When they see you incorporate the input into your behavior and decisions, you seem more approachable. In fact, when my coaching clients practice this question over time, it's not uncommon for them to discover that members of their team begin to ask for and use the input of others as well. (Remember the power of modeling the way?)

Acknowledging and Owning Mistakes

It is amazingly painful for some people to acknowledge a mistake. This is usually because they associate a mistake with their sense of identity and value rather than as a decision or action they could learn from and do differently next time.

Others will acknowledge a mistake but not own the consequences of it. They'll admit spilling the milk but don't feel responsible for cleaning it up.

When people see their leaders both acknowledge a mistake (everyone usually already knows it was a mistake) and then own and address the consequences of it, it gives permission for them to acknowledge their mistakes. Instead of needing to hide them, they can come to you or the team for help.

Psychological safety can be built relatively quickly with most people. We tend to begin relationships openly and are willing to trust. Most of the work should be focused on helping people stay engaged even when they feel vulnerable.

However, some people have difficult pasts where trust was broken. Perhaps that difficult past was with you. In these situations, psychological safety may be difficult to build or rebuild. It will take time. When I'm coaching leaders through rebuilding trust with each other, my assumption is that at least a year of relating differently will be needed. I encourage patience and grace in these situations.

That being said, I have seen many relationships rebuild. My book *Conflict and Leadership* provides additional insights and tools on that topic.

2. Strengthen Self-Determination and Competence

There are three areas that a leader can focus on that help them encourage their team's ability to competently make decisions and act:

a. **Clarify expectations.** If you only fix one thing in your organization, creating clear expectations is it. Lack of clarity is likely the single largest cause of lost effort, unproductivity, conflict, and frustration. At the most basic level, take time to clarify these items:

- Basic roles and responsibilities within the organization (Who is responsible for what?)
- Lines of/scope of authority for each role (Who is responsible for whom?)
- Priorities (What is most important?)

- Indicators of success (How do we measure progress and results?)
- Due dates (When?)

Employees benefit from the minimum effective dose of direct management. Far less management is needed when expectations are clear. And when people know what is expected, they can put all of their effort toward meeting those expectations, not trying to figure out what needs to be done.

b. **Cultivate skills.** Ensure that people's skills match what you ask them to do. Build those skills if they don't already have them. The opportunity for growth is a major driver for employee retention. People like to work where they feel they are growing and are challenged but able to be successful.

Any workplace, any industry can encourage a coaching or mentoring culture. Most are able to provide at least some training opportunities. Many can provide planned growth tracks for their employees.

c. **Nurture confidence.** There are many ways to approach cultivating confidence in others, but probably the most effective is providing people with opportunities where they can succeed at something. People believe their own history.

That was why, in my story about the athlete I was training, I reminded her of her ability to do pull-ups. Pull-ups are not dead lifts—different muscles are involved—but it was an example of her ability to move her bodyweight. She believed it.

If you create psychological safety, clarify expectations and build people's skills, confidence is a likely outcome. Additionally, providing them with opportunities to succeed in new areas also tends to grow confidence.

It's for this reason that when I work with new leaders, they often set goals around personal fitness or getting out of debt. I understand that those goals don't appear to be directly related to job performance, but the confidence that comes from pursuing and achieving those goals will.

PUTTING IT INTO PRACTICE: EXERCISES

- What is one behavior that you can begin to practice that demonstrates the following:
  - Appropriate vulnerability
  - Asking for and engaging with the input of others
  - Acknowledging and owning mistakes

- Think of one person you would like to enable to act:
  - What is one area of expectations that may need to be clarified?
  - What skill might you help them develop? How will you help?
  - What is one success from their past that they may benefit from being reminded of?
  - What is one win you can set them up to accomplish?

Challenge the Process: The Value of Saying What Needs to Be Said

Have you ever noticed how some people become defensive around their workout habits?

When I was growing up, almost everyone used bodybuilding techniques for strength training. It was the way it was done. How can you argue with Arnold? You couldn't. The logic was simple—big muscles made better athletes.

As a high school athlete training for cross-country, track and field, and basketball, bulk was generally not an advantage. In spite of this, our coaches taught techniques designed to build aesthetically pleasing muscle mass. (Because what self-respecting track star doesn't have perfect delts?)

We would put in our reps. Sprinters lifted like long-distance runners who lifted like throwers. We put in real effort. It was better than nothing, but it only tangentially supported performance.

No one questioned the approach. No one challenged the process (even though none of us ever ended up looking like Arnold). It was what people knew. It was how fitness was done. It was either that or leg warmers, tights, and aerobics.

Later, when I became a strength and conditioning instructor, it was at a rock-climbing gym. At that time, most climbers were adamant that climbing was the only way to train for climbing. An elite European climber took this to an extreme by getting others to carry him to climbs out of fear he would add muscle to his legs. This logic was also simple: Strength equals big muscles. Big muscles are heavy. Climbers don't want to be heavy. Climbers shouldn't try to build strength.

Avoiding any kind of cross-training was almost a religious concept, and here I was introducing heresy. I challenged the way things were done. Not on purpose—I didn't get into arguments with people. I just trained differently, and I started leading a class that trained differently.

Personally, I enjoyed cross-training. I wasn't scared of bulking up because I knew that you could be strong without being big. I was interested in longevity and injury mitigation. I thought that there had to be a benefit to working out opposing muscle groups. I also knew that many sport climbers had other interests as well: alpine climbing, endurance racing, skiing, and so on. And many climbers were "tactical athletes" in their real lives—for example, police, firefighters, nurses, and the military. They needed and wanted to do things besides climb plastic holds on a wall.

But some climbers saw what I was doing as an affront. I encountered resistance, but I kept doing my thing. And those who trained with me experienced significant results in their sport climbing. They broke plateaus. Many would advance one or two grades of technical climbing ability within a few months.

Not only that, but soldiers came back from deployments and told me that my training had helped them in the mountains of Afghanistan. Alpinists told me it helped as they pursued Everest, K2, or Denali. Snowboarders told me they noticed a difference on the slopes.

My classes filled until I had to cap attendance. The resistance wavered.

Eventually the gym's youth team started adopting some of my methods. Not coincidentally, this team from a little gym in Alaska began taking home national awards.

The pushback disappeared.

Here's the thing. I never tried to evangelize the climbing "purists." I didn't care how they trained, but it was interesting to me that they cared so much about how other people were training.

The Leadership Parallel

People fall in love with methods.

A method should help you achieve a goal, but many beloved methods don't. Or they don't do it that well. Or they used to, but they don't anymore.

Instead, the method itself becomes the goal.

Leaders and organizations have often developed ways of doing things. Some of these ways were once the best way to do things but no longer are. Some are just preferences—for a variety of reasons—but they don't produce a good return. And some just make us feel good.

This year, a client told me that in their industry a 4% profit margin was the norm. And he's right—that is what that industry tells itself. He went further to say that to even try to improve on that margin would mean they couldn't be competitive. That's because he viewed profitability entirely as a function of pricing. I couldn't persuade him differently. He's stuck. Unless he changes, he won't be able to lead change.

Meanwhile, another client (similar size business, in the same industry, targeting similar clients) routinely does better than 20% in profits. When I began with them, they had been losing money for several years. Yes, they needed competitive pricing. But they became profitable through becoming more effective and efficient in operations. They shifted away from "how things have always been done around here" *to the way things need to be done now.* Those specific changes produced dramatic results that have been sustained over years.

Challenge the Process

Today, I had a conversation with a contractor who will take a 20% loss on their invoicing for a project. The reason? Because they have a habit of waiting for a project to start before ordering supplies. That used to work. Supplies were available locally or could be delivered quickly.

Unfortunately, supply chain issues have meant that the local supply is lean. As opposed to receiving orders in days, it can often take an additional one to two months of delivery time. The contractor has known this for over a year, but they haven't changed their processes. This means they are preventively late on projects—which is costing them.

I pointed out that they could correct this simply by starting their project prep earlier. The general manager pushed back, saying, "I see it differently." He's welcome to a different view, but as Dr. Phil asks, "How is that working for you?"

Many leaders refuse to rethink *how* they do their work. These are leaders who show up regularly, put in their reps, and hope for results. They are smart. They are committed. They are putting in the effort. They are often required to put in too much effort. They experience some level of success, but they are also frustrated by a ceiling on that success: Certain problems keep repeating, or certain opportunities never quite open up. They just accept their version of 4% profits. They insist that no other option is possible.

In many cases, their process is what needs to be challenged. And that can be difficult. People become very comfortable and attached to the way they do things.

- Perhaps the way they do things used to work.
- Maybe they were taught to do things this way by someone they deeply respect.
- Possibly they prefer to avoid the discomfort of being challenged or doing something new or unfamiliar.

Ask yourself, Do your processes work toward or against your goals? Is the way you approach things creating future problems down the road? Are there better ways to go about doing things?

When and How Do You Challenge the Process?

It has been said that leadership is about doing the right things. Management is about doing things right.

The challenge for many leaders—and teams—is that useful, constructive conversation about *both* is often avoided. They tend to talk about one or the other.

Some people satisfy themselves with pursuing the "right" things and assume all efforts in that direction are equal—nonprofits are notorious for this. Others satisfy themselves with "doing things right" and assume that what they are doing is producing the desired results. But they don't check to see if the results are there. When they find that they aren't, the tendency is to point fingers at anything other than *how* they did things.

Leaders should be prepared to challenge the process in these two situations:

- When results are less than what is reasonably expected
- When efforts, investments, or risks are higher than is reasonably expected

Understand the norms for your industry or space. You should be able to match those.

Challenge the process again if either of these situations occurs:

- Results are similar to the norms.
- Efforts, investments, or risks are similar to the norms.

Don't accept industry norms. Most players in your space are underperforming. The norm reflects underperformance.

Caveat—don't challenge every process all the time. That becomes exhausting, and you'll irritate everyone. (Ask me how I know.) Instead, identify the one or two processes that have the biggest impact on your goals.

The Typical Areas That Benefit from Being Challenged

Results. Don't accept 4% profits (or whatever results you seek) just because they are the norm. Look for exceptions that demonstrate how you could do better.

Mindsets. Individuals get stuck in mental frameworks of presuppositions. Groups do as well. Challenge assumptions, especially ones that have universal statements: "We can't." "No one does." Find effective leaders who produce results and who are willing to think and do things differently. Let how they think influence you.

Policies. Policies are rarely designed to help an organization stay in alignment with its values and vision and accomplish its goals. Most are cut-and-paste or reactively built in response to a real or hypothetical problem. That means policy is defined by unchallenged "norms" or fear or problems (disguised as risk mitigation), not by the desired vision and results. Review policy to ensure it propels you forward.

Processes. Many organizations have unclear or undefined processes. Others have overly restrictive ones. (For simplicity's sake, processes are the steps taken for any repeated activity in your organization: hiring, financial reporting, security, maintenance, etc.) Similar to policies, your processes should help you accomplish your values, vision, and goals. Minimally, they shouldn't create friction for them.

People. To paraphrase author and management consultant Jim Collins, the right people need to be in the right seats of the bus."[46] For different reasons, both large and small organizations tend to be too slow to do this, but many problems are resolved just by getting the right people on board and giving them the right job.

Three Methods for Challenging the Process
Demonstration. This is the method I used with the fitness class. I just did it. My approach required very little from anyone else. Anyone who didn't like what I was doing could just ignore me. But the results became evident and spoke for themselves. Demonstration works when you have *visibility* and *autonomy* and when *you can move forward with little buy-in required.*

Demonstration doesn't work if no one can see what you are doing (or the results), if you don't have the freedom to just do things differently, or if you need/should have buy-in.

Identification and suggestion. Identification and suggestion work well when the problem is readily agreed on and there is little debate about the value of change. The problem here is that people usually feel too busy to do the work of change. In this instance, present a first-draft suggestion, which will help focus the attention of others because you've done the heavy lifting.

You'll increase the likelihood of success with this process if your initial suggestion is presented as a first draft that is open to input, edits, and changes. When you present it this way, challenges or questions from others are more likely to be about specific elements of your suggestion—not the suggestion as a whole.

If you suggest something that feels finished, it tends to come across as an imposition or a demand to others, even if it isn't. It increases the likelihood that they might reject it entirely.

Engagement and persuasion. Engagement and persuasion often require more effort, but the results or momentum is more easily sustained. It is often the best approach.

Follow these steps:

1. **Establish the value.**
   a. Clarify how a problem is caused by the current status quo.
   b. Identify the likely value or benefit of improvement. This needs to be significant and compelling *to the people you hope to persuade.*

2. **Get engagement.**
   a. Work with key stakeholders to analyze the problem and develop a solution.
   b. Generate specific commitment to action.

3. **Be accountable.**
   a. Commit to transparently reviewing progress and results with stakeholders.
   b. Commit to adjusting as needed in the future.

Whatever approach is used, a technique that often makes change a more palatable pill to swallow is to frame it like this:

"Let's do X as an experiment for [set time period]. Then we will meet again and determine if it is producing the results we want. At that time, we'll decide if we want to continue what we are doing, stop it, or change it in some way."

That statement works for three reasons:

- The word "experiment" lets people know that this is a learning process.
- The set time period (which should be as short as possible but long enough to generate results) lets people know the experiment can come to an end at some point if it doesn't work.
- The agreement to re-evaluate at that time reduces the risk of commitment for those who feel cautious. They see that there's a way to fix it or revert if needed.

PUTTING IT INTO PRACTICE: EXERCISES

- Identify a simple process problem that is widely recognized but others haven't fixed.
  - Determine which method for challenging the process may be most effective.
  - In a few sentences, write your plan for implementing that method.
  - What challenges might you anticipate?
  - How will you address those challenges if they occur?
  - What help do you need?
  - When will you start?

CHAPTER 16

Encourage the Heart: What Distinguishes Truly Great Leaders

You get the best effort from others not by lighting a fire beneath them, but by building a fire within. — Bob Nelson

When I competed in my first BJJ tournament, I was a bundle of nerves. I prepared as hard as I could, but I was beaten twice: first by submission and the second time by the judges' decision.

I didn't have fun. The nerves weren't fun. Getting beat wasn't fun. Nothing was fun. Besides, I was in my 40s. What business did I have getting involved in competition with guys in their 20s? Why do this to myself?

I didn't want to admit it to anyone, but I was done with tournaments. They were not for me. Then I had a conversation about my experience with an experienced BJJ practitioner. He was formerly in the Marines—Force Recon.

"I felt the same way my first few tournaments," he said. This surprised me. Why would someone accustomed to war feel like this about a simple tournament?

He continued, "It took me about four tournaments to find my groove and get comfortable. You might do the same. Do four or so tournaments, get past the nerves and then decide if this is for you or not."

I felt encouraged. I also looked at tournaments differently afterward. Instead of approaching them from a perspective of "What do I need to do to win?" I approached them from a perspective of "How can tournaments teach me to keep my head in the game under stress?" I realized that overcoming the head game was more important and more valuable than beating an opponent.

In my next tournament, I stopped worrying about winning or losing. I focused on my goal: "Keep my head and stay intentional with every movement."

To my surprise, I won.

And that tournament was fun.

What Is Encouragement?

Encouraging the heart, for leaders, is mostly about helping your people win their head games. Successful encouragement helps accomplish two things: it builds connection or community, and it helps others achieve results.

The English word "encourage" comes from the 15th-century French word *encoragier*, meaning "to make strong, to hearten."[47] The English construction literally means "to put courage into."

In my story above, I had lost heart for competition. And someone put that heart back into me. They encouraged me. They didn't tell me I did well, didn't point out my strengths, and didn't say anything nice about me. They didn't even say "You can do it."

Encouragement is not about making people feel better or making them feel good. Those are side effects. People feel good when they feel connected to others and when they are accomplishing goals.

My encourager connected with me: "I was there too." Then he reframed the goal.

Leadership, in general, is a soft skill. *Encouraging the heart* can seem like the softest of those skills. Of the five leadership strengths that I describe in this book, it's my opinion that *inspiring a shared vision* is the strength that most distinguishes someone as a leader. But it's the ability to *encourage the heart* that is most strongly correlated with overall leadership effectiveness.

Three Ingredients for Successful Encouragement

The "well dones" and slaps on the back are fine—don't stop. But for encouragement that builds and sustains high morale, you need to go deeper. This includes three things: psychological safety, alignment, and adjusting how you measure progress.

Psychological Safety (a.k.a. Trust)

We discussed this earlier, but I'll make two short new observations here. Harvard researcher, Amy Edmondson, coined the term *psychological safety.* This observation emerged from studying high-performing teams in hospitals. She discovered that teams that scored low in terms of psychological safety tended to have higher rates of error and malpractice.

For example, a surgeon has a strong command capacity in their leadership. If nurses feel uncomfortable pointing out a problem or asking a question, the surgeon's error rates increase, and errors are harder to correct in a timely way. However, if a surgeon creates an environment where nurses feel they can speak up, error rates decline.[48]

This observation was further supported from internal research within Google called Project Aristotle. Google found that their highest-performing teams weren't the ones with the smartest or most individually competent members. Instead, it was the teams that had a sense of psychological safety.[49]

People gain courage and perform higher when they trust their team and their leaders.

Alignment

Well-aligned teams that have a similar way of approaching shared values, vision, or priorities find a sense of connection, of community. Building alignment within an organization is valuable for many reasons, one of which is simply that people like it better. It's encouraging to know you are working *with* others, not just *beside* or, worse, *against.*

This contributes to psychological safety as well, because the more alignment there is, the more likely it is that there is a common sense of values, purpose, and direction.

Adjusting How We Measure Progress

I believe in using good metrics and tracking progress, but at times this creates unanticipated problems. As it relates to encouraging the heart, I want to address some of these.

Being absolutist about success. I once led a nonprofit. We had set a stretch goal for ourselves, and when the year ended, we hadn't completed the goal. I felt discouraged and a little defeated. It took a while before I realized that even though we hadn't accomplished the stretch goal, it had still been our best year ever.

Instead of looking at the ground we'd actually covered, I was fixated on the gap between where we were and the goal. It was absolutist thinking—all or nothing. It didn't help.

Not recognizing effort. My son recently competed in a BJJ tournament. He was equally matched with his opponent. They both fought hard and well. One person's attack was skillfully negated by the other's defense. At the end of what looked like an exhausting match, neither had been able to score a point.

Naming a winner came down to the judge's decision. He chose my son's opponent. I could understand why. While unsuccessful, that boy had attempted more attacks than my son. My son was discouraged by this. He wasn't rewarded for his effort.

I'm not a fan of participation medals. As far as I'm concerned, my son's real reward was the experience. He fought, did his best, and held off a worthy opponent. It's good for him to learn that he can get beat. That lesson will make him harder to beat next time.

But effort matters. I made sure to recognize his. I pointed out all of the things he did right. He didn't get the outcome he wanted this time, but he is more likely to in the future if he keeps putting in the right effort. More importantly, he's learning to face a challenge and continue through difficulty and resistance. That lesson, on its own, is more important than winning a match. I don't want him to lose that lesson.

Many good leaders are results oriented. Results matter, but people can do their best and still not accomplish what they hoped for. Or they make a mistake. It's important that we keep an eye on their future wins and accomplishments.

Recognize the effort people put in. If they don't succeed, help them understand what can be learned. Encourage them to keep showing up to put in more effort.

PUTTING IT INTO PRACTICE: EXERCISES

1. Identify encouraging behaviors:
   - Think of one specific person who helped you see your value and gave you courage to try something you otherwise might not have tried. This might be a parent, teacher, mentor, or employer of some kind.
   - Make a list of specific ways that describe how they generally related to you and others. What were their typical attitudes? How did they tend to speak to (or about) others? How did they behave and relate? Try to identify at least 10 ways of relating that really stand out to you.
   - After you've completed your list, make a check mark by each item that contributed toward you feeling more confident to act, contribute, participate, say, or try something that you otherwise might not have.
   - Underline one to three that seemed to be the most meaningful to you.

What do you learn from this list? Which of their ways of relating are now a part of your regular way of relating to those you lead?

2.   Encourage someone else:

Is there someone in your sphere of influence who would benefit from being encouraged?

In what one way might you relate to them to produce encouragement? (This may or may not come from the list above.)

When and where do you think you could express encouragement toward that person? Here is how to do it:

- **Identify something you want to encourage.** This could be effort, attitude, or an accomplishment.
- **Tell them.** Mention a specific area of strength that they have.
- **Identify progress they've made.** Focus on what they've done well in terms of growing in that strength or exercising it. Don't focus on or mention any gaps that remain. (There is a place for those conversations, but have this one without trying to help or coach them.)
- **Recognize the effort.** Let people know that you recognize their hard work or appreciate their attention to detail or value their timeliness. This is a focus on *how* they work, not on the results. Identify strengths in terms of how they work.
- **Describe impact or value.** Help people see the value they bring. This is especially important for people in support roles who often have a more difficult time understanding how they directly contribute to the success of the whole.

A formula for the conversation might look like this: describe the strength, recognize the effort, and describe the impact.

How to encourage following a "win"
"I wanted to let you know I really appreciated how well you organized the workshop. You have a real ability to manage logistics and details. Your

work helps everyone feel comfortable and allows me to focus on delivering the presentation."

How to encourage following a "loss"
"I wanted to let you know I really appreciated your hard work on that proposal. As you know, we didn't win it, but it was well written, thorough, and descriptive, and the estimates were fair. In fact, we received feedback that it was one of the most clearly written proposals submitted. Even though we didn't win this one, it helped us stand out to the client, and they have invited additional proposals in the future."

POWER: DECISIVENESS, SPEED, AND MOMENTUM

Power is of two kinds. One is obtained by the fear of punishment and the other by acts of love. Power based on love is a thousand times more effective and permanent then the one derived from fear of punishment. — Mahatma Gandhi[50]

CHAPTER 17

Introduction to Power

Sports that require power have a visceral appeal. Watching a power-lifter, gymnast, or wrestler overcome and move through incredible resistance can be captivating. Even in team sports that don't focus on individual power, we are captivated by powerful moments: hitting a home run, slam-dunking, or smashing through a defensive line.

The demonstration of power in sports like these is one of the most overt examples of making something happen that doesn't want to happen. A 1,000-pound barbell is normally inert. The human body doesn't naturally flip itself through the air. An opposing wrestler doesn't volunteer to be taken down. What isn't always obvious is the level of skill, technique, and control that is usually required.

Power, defined technically, is force multiplied by distance divided by time.[51] Simply, how quickly can strength be delivered? The more strength available to an athlete and the faster they can access that strength to move themselves (or something else), the more powerful they are.

Strength, on its own, can move something. Power (strength + speed) is different in that it creates momentum. It propels. This correlates to leadership as well. A leader acts powerfully when they harness their strengths to quickly achieve substantive results. Most leaders have power intrinsic to their position—the ability to write a check, to make decisions, to hire or fire. Some leaders don't have that kind of power, but they do have influence.

Not everything can or should be done quickly or powerfully. But there are times when the leader's use of power is needed and is the only correct answer. Times of conflict, change and crisis are often times when power is needed.

A WARNING ABOUT POWER

Power can be destructive, especially when applied too often or with poor timing or ineffective methods or the wrong purposes. This is the Machiavellian approach to leadership, which primarily focuses on the accumulation, use, and defense of power. While I don't subscribe to this approach, it's worth being familiar with it because many people lead from this perspective.

Getting the balance right is difficult for many leaders. Some err by using power too much. Others err by not using it enough.

Brazilian jiu-jitsu can be similar for new practitioners who are strong. They will often try to overcome their lack of skill with power. The result is that they tend to injure themselves and others. (In the BJJ community, it's often said that the most dangerous practitioners are the new ones.)

On the other hand, some new people—especially if they don't see themselves as strong—will not be powerful when they need to be. They may not have developed the necessary underlying strength. They may feel shy about being physically assertive. They may not know how to effectively apply power.

POWER IS NECESSARY

It can be intimidating to some. It can be intoxicating to others. Both intimidation and intoxication can create problems for leaders. The solution to managing either is to ensure that our focus is not on ourselves but on those we serve. Leadership based on the exercise of power is leader-first leadership. This is true regardless of what a leader says or possibly, even believes.

One of the many downsides of power-based leadership is that it tends to focus on the accumulation and defense of power. Other people are used to that end. Actual leadership is perceived as a means to power, not a role of service. This is an important difference.

Leaders who are afraid of losing their power will tend to unnecessarily create situations where their power appears to be needed. This allows for demonstrations of power (and their sense of worth) but it is nearly always at a cost to those supposedly being served.

Power—like money or fame—is a magnifier. It doesn't tend to change or corrupt people. Instead, it tends to magnify the core character of the person.

When leading in the context of conflict, change or crisis a leader will need to overcome both passive inertia and active resistance. Leaders who do not act powerfully will find themselves coming up short when leadership is needed the most. Leaders who misapply their power will find themselves harming their chances of success and possibly others.

I'll focus specifically on the three common areas where leadership often needs to be powerful.

CHAPTER 18

Conflict: The Opportunity for Improvement

onflict. It's not *if*; it's *when*. In spite of the frequency with which conflict is experienced, it still takes many leaders by surprise. This chapter provides a high-level overview of the topic. For a deeper understanding, I recommend that you read my book *Conflict and Leadership*.

THE FITNESS ANALOGY

Almost if not all sports have a conflict. If it isn't a competition between teams or individuals, it's a fight against physics or personal resolve. In sports these conflicts are assumed, expected, and even wanted. That's why sportsmanship is (usually) taught, respected, and awarded.

However, within teams and organizations, conflict often comes as an unwanted surprise. Leaders often don't know what to do when this occurs. Common tendencies are to try to avoid the issue and hope it goes away or attack the people involved. Neither approach is effective.

Conflict is considered a power move in leadership because it often requires the fast or intensive application of all the previously discussed leadership strengths. Because of the potential for harm, it also requires incredible control.

WHAT IS CONFLICT?

Conflict is a disagreement over something important to two or more people. That seems obvious. But what we tend to overlook is the "something important to two or more." The tendency is to think, "This is important to me. They are stupid."

Understanding what is important to others is the key to unlocking conflict.

CONFLICT AS AN OPPORTUNITY

Conflict is an opportunity. If we understand this, our leadership can move to an entirely new level. When most leaders think of conflict, they think about two people on the team who are fighting, an unhappy customer, a contract dispute, or that employee who needs to be confronted or reprimanded.

Each of those may be conflict scenarios, but they are often symptoms rather than causes. Conflict within organizations often is rooted somewhere other than where the symptoms appear. If you know how to identify it, it's easier to resolve. A key problem for most leaders is a misdiagnosis of the cause of conflict.

Part of this is because we tend to think that conflict looks a certain way. But conflict isn't always emotional and red in the face. It might be cold. It might be silent. It might have a smile and flattering words. It might not be easy to recognize.

It often looks different from what you think; for example, consider high staff turnover, lower profits, cash flow issues, increased workers' comp claims, or difficulty retaining repeat business. These are all indicators that *something* isn't working right. Frequently, conflict is part of that something.

And this is why conflict is valuable. It tells us that there is something we need to take a look at. It provides us with an area to focus on, which, if improved, often not only resolves the conflict but also improves organizational performance as a whole.

THE FOUR OPPORTUNITIES OF CONFLICT

Conflict manifests within four different spheres of organizational reality:

- Organizational culture
- Systems and structures
- Relationships
- Individual or personal dynamics

When conflict is first recognized in an organization, it usually manifests on the relational or personal level. That's why almost all books about conflict resolution focus on the interpersonal dynamics of conflict.

But the majority of the time, what is really happening is that individuals or relationships are reacting to cultural or system-and-structure issues.

ORGANIZATIONAL CULTURE

Organizational culture is a fancy way of describing commonly practiced *behaviors* and *decisions* that are derived from commonly held *values* that are derived from commonly held *beliefs*.

As a young mediator, I used to spend months with teams helping them untangle and straighten out all the threads of their relationship issues. That's how I was trained, and it worked. It was labor-intensive and exhausting, but it worked.

Over time, I began to notice that frontline team dynamics were mirrors of their management. I referred to this dynamic in the earlier discussion of modeling the way. Management, in turn, tended to mirror a dynamic at the executive and board levels. That is evidence of culture.

For example, consistently responsive and respectful customer service from the frontline employees is nearly always modeled by their management. If this customer service experience is similar across the company, it's an indication that whoever manages the managers also values, teaches, and models this.

Conversely, if frontline staff tend to be conflict averse and avoid accountability, you will probably find the same dynamics with their managers. If this is common within management, it is likely common with their leaders. Again, it's a reflection of values, teaching, and modeling.

The stronger a culture is, the more commonality there is at each level. Leaders *always* set the tone for the culture of their organizations. The stronger an individual leader is, the more the culture is a reflection of that leader.

If similar kinds of issues occur across the organization, there is a good chance that culture might be part of the issue. Cultural problems are diverse and can include tendencies such as avoidance of conflict, disrespect, disregard for the safety or health of others, perfectionism, "never enough," "get what you can," and so on.

Power move. Senior leaders are the creators or interpreters of culture (See "Individual and Personal Dynamics" below.) Issues within an organizational culture often reflect the leaders' own personal values or preferences in some way. The power move is to get honest and ask two questions:

- How might my beliefs, values, or behaviors be driving this issue?
- In what ways might my beliefs, values, or behaviors need to change?

Often there is a need to get outside help—someone from outside the culture who takes an objective look.

That isn't easy, as we discussed earlier—*you lead out of who you are.*

SYSTEMS AND STRUCTURES

Systems refer to how the dots are connected within your organization. It can be a guiding policy. It can be a step-by-step process or procedure. Structures might even be more concrete, like office layouts or organizational structures (organigrams).

If problems tend to occur repeatedly and especially at certain times, places, events, or with certain people, it's possible that it is a systems or structure problem. In many cases, you'll find that there was insufficient clarity in the systems. In some cases, improving the physical environment is all that is needed.

Examples:

- **Action items.** The simple practice of assigning action items at the end of every meeting, with a clearly defined *who* is responsible for *what* by *when* solves a lot of problems. The follow-up practice of reviewing these items at the beginning of each meeting solves many of the remaining problems.
- **Accounting and management.** I've often been told, "We can't do this because our accounting system isn't set up for it." That is the tail wagging the dog. The accounting system serves the needs of the organization. Not the other way around.

Power move. The power move is to accurately identify what is triggering the conflict. In some cases, something that seemed good might need to be changed.

For growing organizations, this often means formalizing something that used to be comfortably informal. For large organizations, this can include remembering that the systems and structures (bureaucracy, software, etc.) are intended to serve the purpose of the organization and not to be served *by* it.

You know something could be systemic or structural if it is regularly experienced, especially when it is experienced at a consistent time, place, event, or between roles.

RELATIONSHIPS

Relational issues are what most people think about when they think of conflict. These tend to break down into two basic types of disputes: *substantive* and *personal*.

- **Substantive disputes.** These are about a thing: how, what, when, where, who. For example, a disagreement about which vender to hire, or a budget priority, or a strategic priority.
- **Personal disputes.** These are about character. Trust and respect typically are major players in this space. For example, "He always lies." "She is lazy and can't be counted on."

Between the two, substantive disputes are the easiest to resolve, especially if they aren't personalized at all. But a substantive dispute can easily become personal. The substantive issue of someone being late on a project a couple of times can easily turn into a personalized interpretation that "he isn't reliable." (It may be that he wasn't given the resources he needed, the expectations were unrealistic, etc.)

There are a number of tools for resolving relational conflicts—conflicts that you are involved in as well as ones that you are coaching someone through. Again, I go into those in greater depth in *Conflict and Leadership*.

Power move. The power move is engaging with the issue. Most people avoid wading into the mix, but for those (like me) who tend to go there, the power move is knowing how to hold back. Sometimes my impatience or discomfort with unresolved issues motivates me to push too hard and too forcefully for resolution. Practicing patience and restraint can be helpful.

Here is a simple framework that—when followed with an attitude of humility and self-reflection—tends to go a long way toward helping *most* disputes:

1. **Clarify what you really want.**
   Ask yourself:

- What does "fixing" this look like to me? What does an acceptable solution look like?
- Who do I want to be? How do I want to behave during this dispute? (What are my highest values, and how can I be consistent with them?)

In most disputes that I've worked with, people tend not to have a clear understanding of what a solution might look like for them. As a result, they are unable to work toward resolution.

Additionally, most people will say "I feel respect or honesty are my highest values." It is easy to insist that the other party treat us with respect and that they be honest. But integrity means that we also are careful to relate to the other person respectfully, be honest, or listen to someone else's honest feedback.

2. **Own your part.**

Ask yourself:

- Is there anything I've done (or not done) that was perceived as meaningful to the other person (even if not meaningful to me)?
- Is there any way I've acted that is out of alignment with my highest values?

If both people can take ownership of their roles in the dispute, the whole situation can often be resolved relatively quickly. Even if only one person will take ownership, resolution is more likely.

Unfortunately, the tendency is for both to point at the other party and say, "Anything I might have done wrong was entirely justified by whatever they did wrong." This attitude tends to keep things stuck in a stalemate.

What reliably works is when one party says, "I acknowledge that I did A, B, or C, and it had this or that impact on you." Even if their part really was only 10% of the problem, it tends to unlock the issue. The other party will often reciprocate and say, "Okay, well, I admit that I could have done X, Y, or Z differently."

3. **Ask for what you want.**
    Ask yourself:
    *   Am I willing to articulate what "fixing this" might look like?
    *   Am I prepared to consider (and offer) options or alternatives?

It seems obvious, but many people never say what they want. They just sit in their dissatisfaction and believe that the other side should be able to read their mind. Or they'll put an offer out there, but it isn't what they really wanted.

I've mediated litigated cases where a party was suing for hundreds of thousands of dollars but really wanted an authentic apology from the other side.

If we aren't willing to say what we want, we have to be prepared for the possibility that the other side might be trying to resolve things with us in complete good faith but just isn't a good-enough guesser to figure out what we are thinking.

4. **Be willing to let go.**
    Ask yourself:
    *   Am I willing / how do I let go if there is resolution?
    *   Am I willing / how do I let go if there isn't resolution (or there's only partial resolution)?

Letting go of a dispute can be difficult for many people. That is a large topic by itself. To keep it simple: If we believe someone has wronged us and we hold on to that emotion, it consumes some of our mental and emotional energy. Taken to an extreme, resentment, anger, frustration, and so on can affect us physically as well.

There have been times when I've been wronged at work: Perhaps a client wouldn't pay, or a contractor didn't follow through. For my own peace of mind, it was more important to let it go than to keep pursuing the issue.

Letting it go doesn't mean not remembering the issue anymore. It doesn't necessarily mean restoring trust completely to the person either. It also doesn't always mean that there weren't any consequences (asking for what you wanted might have included consequences for yourself or others).

It does mean four things:

- Committing not to "chew on" the issue
- Agreeing not to bring it up with others—no gossiping about it
- Agreeing not to use it against someone at a later date
- Being open to the reconciliation of the relationship *if* the other person acknowledges their part

Relational disputes are typically obvious, but the most difficult ones to address are the ones with conflict-avoidant and nice people. Look for breakdowns in the quality of communication and trust.

INDIVIDUAL AND PERSONAL DYNAMICS

This refers to how we interpret and relate to conflict when it occurs. It also has to do with values or behavioral patterns that contribute to conflicts.

We all learn to interpret and relate to conflict over the course of our lives. Most of us learned that conflict is somehow bad. It represents the end of something, often a relationship, a good experience, or an opportunity. However, how we relate to that can vary. Some of us lean toward avoiding conflicts. Others lean toward winning the conflict. Flight or fight.

Additionally, many leaders don't even recognize that their personal way of relating is creating the conditions for conflict. For example, some leaders are driven to rescue or be the hero in situations. This looks like firefighting and needing to fix things all the time. It also means that they either create dynamics where fires are easily started *or* refuse to improve dynamics so that there are fewer fires.

Classic type A personalities may push so hard for decisions and results that they never really build consensus. Or they don't embrace true deliberation. This approach avoids or skips past healthy conflict. As a result, it doesn't go away. It just reemerges downstream.

Power move. The power move is self-development. This might mean therapy or coaching. It means being willing to honestly explore ownership whenever there are cultural or system-and-structure conflicts. For some leaders, it means learning to address conflict in a timely way. For others, it means learning to exercise an appropriate amount of restraint. For nearly all, it requires redefining conflict away from "bad" or "wrong" to "opportunity."

PUTTING IT INTO PRACTICE: EXERCISES

- Identify a small conflict that you are experiencing at home or at work. (Start with a small one if you can.)
- Determine which one or more of the power moves seem most relevant to this conflict.
- Outline your plan for using those principles to address the conflict.
- Determine if you need help in this process. Who could help you? In what way?

Leading Change: Engaging Hearts and Minds

One of the most important power moves for leaders is the ability to lead change well. In a sense, this is what all leadership is about. Growth, adjustments to circumstances, pursuing opportunities, or addressing challenges all require leadership and all are forms of change.

The kind of change addressed in this chapter is not organic, evolutionary change. We're talking about hard right-hand turns or complete turn-arounds. Very often, this includes significant changes in growth, direction, strategy, structure, methods, or dynamics.

Effective leaders are intentional and purposeful with change. They don't avoid it. They don't change for the sake of novelty. But they identify needed areas for change and pursue them.

In fitness, a change in training regimen is part of how both growth and recovery are stimulated.

In the fitness world, it has become common to constantly introduce change into many training programs. This is particularly true for classes or methods that are focused on the general public or on fat loss. This is because frequent change prevents the body from finding homeostasis. This results in higher calorie burn. Additionally, change is novel. It is easier to fill classes with people who are just trying to stay in shape and get bored easily. The goals are calorie burn and client retention.

But fitness programs that are designed to build deep strength, power, or skill *do not* introduce frequent or random change. Powerlifters, gymnasts, basketball teams, runners, or any athlete focused on performance will practice the same movements and drills over and over. They'll do this to increase their efficiency and skill. For these athletes, change is carefully designed into the program, then led. They seek performance-related goals.

The appropriateness of either approach is dependent on your goals. However, in both approaches, the best kind of change is planned and intentional.

STEPS TO LEAD ANY KIND OF CHANGE EFFECTIVELY

As mentioned earlier, the core strengths of leadership—particularly being able to inspire a shared vision—are critical in change. You may also find yourself dipping into the last chapter on conflict. The following outline will help guide your change process:

1. Ensure that you have credibility.

Change creates uncertainty. The future is unknown. When leaders are highly trusted, it is easier for them to lead change. When leaders haven't earned sufficient trust or have lost it, leading change will be more difficult.

For leaders to be viewed as fully credible, people need to be able to offer an unqualified yes to the three following questions:

- Do I believe this leader cares about me/us?
- Do I believe this leader is trustworthy (has integrity or will do what they say they will do)?
- Do I believe this leader is competent and able to do the job?

Think of any leader who has successfully led a change process *and* was broadly supported by those around them. My guess is that people believed that the leader cared for them, was trusted, and was viewed as competent.

Now think of a leader who struggled to lead or sustain a change process, especially if a major part of the problem was a lack of engagement or even active resistance from others. I expect that you'll find that a significant portion of their constituency answered no to one or more of the questions above.

This brings us to a tricky reality: Perception matters. Being caring and being trustworthy and competent matters. But others must perceive you this way. If they don't, you don't have credibility.

2. ID core issues, or target the change.

Well-defined problems are easier to solve. Well-defined targets are easier to hit. Many teams and leaders get lost in a maze when they don't clearly define their issues or goals.

Clearly define what is motivating change. This might be a problem or an opportunity, internal or external.

This should include the why of change. What is the benefit of this change, particularly for those being asked to produce or support it? You will probably never overcommunicate this. But many leaders under-communicate it, assuming that everyone already understands.

I have found that framing these core issues as questions helps create a tight focus. It also leverages people's natural tendency to see questions as things that have answers.

For example, imagine a situation where an office is struggling with staff tardiness. The issues might be that staff show up late or supervisors aren't holding staff accountable. These aren't inaccurate. But the way they are framed doesn't generate momentum.

Reframe these as questions:

- How can we ensure staff will show up on time?
- How can we help supervisors to hold staff accountable?

In another situation where one business has acquired another, the issues may be retaining the acquired company's management team or that their customers won't accept a change in ownership. Reframe this:

- How do we retain their management team?
- How do we communicate with and engage their customers?

Reframing with questions like these more naturally leads to action.

3. Communicate "Why" not methods

The engineer who designs a bridge would love to talk to you about the engineering challenges they overcame with their design. The driver who uses the bridge couldn't care less and never thinks about those things. They just want to know, "Does it go where I want to go?"

When discussing the need for change, focus on where you are going, especially the value it will bring. You need to know how to get there, just as the engineer needs to be able to design a reliable bridge and the contractor needs to know how to build it.

When talking to people who will be affected by the change but whose involvement isn't necessary to produce the change, just explaining why is often enough.

When engaging people whose support you need to make the change, you may need to discuss and determine how, but keep reminding them of why. It's the job of the leader to not let people lose sight of the forest for the trees. The easiest way to engage them is to involve them in shaping the methods, as I mentioned earlier when discussing vision.

People tend to get mired down in how. Often, this is due to forgetting why. In many cases, getting how 100% correct is less important than getting it to a place of *good enough*.

4. Clearly define success.

Create metrics that will indicate when change has been completed. Some changes, like moving offices, are relatively obvious. Other changes, like improving quality and consistency in production, can be ambiguous if not clearly defined. Either way, define what success or winning will look like. There is rarely a clearly defined tape across the finish line of a change process, so you need to create one.

5. Act/follow through regularly.

This will help everyone to track progress and determine the quality of results. (Was the change process worth it?) Additionally, it will help keep you from wandering away from the change effort before it is completed because it feels as if a lot of work was done.

Leaders sabotage their own success (and credibility) if they make a big ask (or demand) of others but either don't contribute at their end or don't work to follow through.

6. Identify mileposts in the road.

Make sure that your and your team's decisions, actions, and habits are in alignment with the change you are pursuing. It is easy to become tired or distracted on the road to change.

When I was 10, my family packed up a converted school bus and moved to Alaska. Once we hit the Alcan (Alaska–Canada) Highway, we started referring to a book called *The Milepost*.

Because the distances were so vast and the roads were so long and the signage so unreliable, narrow green markers along the highway numbered each mile. These mileposts helped us track progress and orient ourselves. That helped with everything: planning side trips, making stops, deciding where and when we should fuel up, and so on.

Change processes are sometimes long, and teams can get lost in the middle of them. Create mileposts for your team to help them see their progress. I usually do this through planning processes that list large multi-year, annual, quarterly, and monthly goals with metrics. However you do it, create frequent enough indicators to help ensure that you are tracking progress. These serve several purposes, including making progress more evident, ensuring that you are moving at the correct pace, allowing for course corrections, and overall accountability.

7. Be prepared for detours and contingencies.

I recently sat down with a client who'd had a challenging year. A number of expected outcomes hadn't occurred, but because of well-defined mileposts, they were able to celebrate. They realized they had made significant progress in many areas. And they knew, based on those mileposts, that the outcomes they sought this year were just around the bend.

When it comes to maintaining my fitness goals, I try to anticipate likely interruptions, opportunities, or challenges. Over the course of a year, the most likely challenges I'll encounter will be trips, injuries, or sickness. The most likely opportunities will be competitions or events I want to participate in.

To the degree that these are foreseeable, I plan my training to accommodate them. I might plan for a recovery week while traveling or plan to visit BJJ schools. If sick or injured, I'll view it as an unplanned recovery opportunity but will also determine what I can still do to help maintain progress toward my desired goals.

Many change processes are journeys, and along the way there are both opportunities and challenges. You can't anticipate all of them. But you can anticipate the likely ones. These may include seasonal changes in your work calendar, times when projects at work will require more attention or less, or foreseeable external changes: economic, technical, regulatory, etc.

Develop a set of scenarios for how you will keep the change process on track in the event of the most likely opportunities or challenges.

8 Celebrate and acknowledge the success of completed change.

Many organizational changes are obvious on paper: "Let's create a customer service culture!" "Let's get more structure around here!" "Everyone should be more accountable!"

But in practice, much of this work is either so incremental or so entwined with other dynamics and issues that the plot can be lost. It is of great value for the leader to keep cheering the team on until the end and—once they've reached that clearly defined end—to acknowledge or celebrate it. Recognize, "Yes, we did this!" And again emphasize the value of what was accomplished.

9. Capture lessons learned.

A practice of capturing lessons learned is generally valuable. It is particularly valuable when it comes to leading change processes. Use this very simple set of questions to do this:

- What did we set out to accomplish?
- What actually happened?
- What went well that we should repeat?
- What should we do differently?

PUTTING IT INTO PRACTICE: EXERCISES

- Think of a change you'd like to implement. Start simple if you've not done this before. Ideally pick a change that can be implemented within a short time frame so that you can quickly see how this whole process works.
- Use the outline above to map out how you will approach the change.
- Implement. Don't forget to review your lessons learned.

CHAPTER 20

Leading in a Crisis: Creating Clarity and Confidence

Senior Master Sergeant Jeremy Maddamma is one of my training partners in Brazilian Jiu-Jitsu. He is a special operator, Air Force Pararescue. On a mission in Afghanistan he was shot in his left knee. After spending a couple of years in and out of surgeries and therapy trying to save his leg, he finally had it removed. After recovery, he requalified to go back to active-duty special operations with one leg and a fancy prosthetic.

Nice guy. A family man. One tough hombre.

Most of his career is about intervening in someone else's crisis. Then he had a crisis. But the crisis hasn't taken him off mission. Crisis changed his path—but not the goal.

Leaders should expect to face crisis. However, not all leaders will relate to crisis the same way. The way you relate to it matters.

WHAT IS A CRISIS?

A crisis is any kind of stressful or acute situation that is—usually—destabilizing, threatening, or damaging, and requires an urgent change or response.

Crisis can come in all kinds of flavors.

A crisis might be your fault. It might be an accident. It might be due to the actions of others. It might be out of anyone's control—like a natural disaster.

It might be perceived. It might be real.

During times of crisis, the sense of need for leadership grows dramatically. However, many leaders stop leading. Instead, they get sucked into reactions: fight, flight, or freeze. Academics will tell you these are survival responses, but in the real world reactive decisions don't often improve your chances of survival.

Take your academic friend in the woods. Encounter a grizzly on the trail. You'll hope that your ivory-towered buddy has better bear sense than his gut reactions. (That being said—whatever your friend's reactions are—just remember: you don't need to be faster than the bear, you just need to be faster than your friend!)

Kidding aside, the power move is to keep your head. It doesn't look like power, but by being able to stay intentional, deliberate, and focused—as opposed to reactive—you are able to create powerful results.

Just because there is a crisis doesn't mean you should be in crisis.

How to Address Most Crises

While each crisis can be wildly different from another, there are basic concepts or principles that help.

Before the Crisis—Prepare

I mentioned Air Force Pararescue. They have one of the longest training pipelines of any special operations group in the United States. Because their primary mission is to rescue other trained military personnel, you can assume that things are very wrong and out of control when they are called in.[52]

They don't get to pick and choose when or where to encounter the enemy. They can't set up safe and secure environments to treat or extract the wounded. They have to be able to enter a crisis and then either control it or safely exit it—along with whomever they are rescuing.

They do this well because of how well they prepare. Because they can't choose their battles, success is dependent on their ability to make the best choices in any given situation. Good preparation includes four steps:

- **Anticipation.** You can't know the future, but you can anticipate likely problem scenarios. There are three reasons why this is an important exercise:

  1. Being able to anticipate problems helps you prevent them from occurring in the first place.

  2. It helps you maintain an active position as opposed to a reactive one—even if things don't go to plan.

  3. It creates more nimble thinking, which helps you recognize and respond to problems *and* opportunities more quickly.

     Basic scenarios planning is taking a look at best-case, worst-case, and most-likely scenarios. There are many other ways to go about this as well. The point is to realize that there are multiple possibilities for how the future could play out and to prepare for the most likely ones.

- **Planning.** After likely scenarios have been identified, plan how you will respond. Don't just adopt someone else's risk management strategy and file it away. The real value of this exercise is the practice of thinking it through.

  Practicing your responses—via planning exercises—will help you think faster and more clearly in a real scenario even if the plan can't work as intended or an unanticipated situation occurs.

- **Action.** Don't stop at planning. Do the work of preparing for the most likely scenarios. Do what you can to mitigate them. Prepare the resources that might be needed.

  I live in Alaska. It's January as I write. The power went out at our house for most of the morning. This knocked the heat out. A cold house in the winter isn't just uncomfortable—it can lead to frozen and burst pipes, which can create further damage to the house. Potentially, it's even life threatening.

Fortunately, we were prepared. We had wood-heating alternatives. I have a backup generator. All of that took anticipation and then action. I had previously upgraded our fireplace so it could heat the house instead of just looking pretty. I had bought a generator and had an electrician install a transfer switch. We had fuel set aside for the generator.

The plan to prepare is meaningless if the preparation doesn't actually happen. Preparation can take a crisis and turn it into a mere inconvenience or even an adventure.

- **Exposure.** When I trained for international disaster relief, we were intentionally deprived of food and sleep and were forced to hike through the Swiss Alps while being confronted with simulated corrupt officials, checkpoints, armed raids, robberies, kidnappings, and so on.

It wasn't real, but it simulated an element of reality. And it did so to a sufficient degree that stress reactions were induced. Roughly 80% of the participants either dropped out, decided this wasn't for them, or weren't invited to go to the field.

When I went to the field, I was never kidnapped. But I frequently dealt with corrupt authorities, and I was stuck at a lot of checkpoints, held at gunpoint numerous times, threatened with imprisonment, trapped between warring tribes, and so on. The simulated exposure was immensely helpful. Even though I had never been through "it" before, when "it" occurred, it felt familiar. Which meant I could focus on handling the situation well as opposed to reacting and making things worse.

Some crises are very emotional, dynamic, and overwhelming—maybe even shocking. Being emotionally prepared through exposing yourself and your team to similar events helps. This is why schools run fire drills or earthquake drills. Now there are active shooter drills.

In anything I've trained in—from sports to foreign language skills to team or leadership exercises—the programs I've gotten the most out of have been the ones where pressure and stress were artificially induced.

Run drills. Have dress rehearsals. Practice scenario games where team members are forced to think through solving a real problem together.

In my opinion, these kinds of exercises are worth far more (in terms of team building) than any ropes course.

DURING THE CRISIS

Gathering and Interpreting Information

During a crisis there is usually (a) not enough reliable or useful information and (b) too much distracting, irrelevant, and untrustworthy information.

The first challenge is telling the two apart. The second, usually, is knowing how to make decisions without enough information.

Determining Reliability or Usefulness

1. **Center on clarity.**

    Clarity rarely creates itself. The more you practice creating clarity in normal times, the easier it will be to create it in a crisis. Developing clarity in three specific areas is key:

    a. **Values.** The clearer you are about your core values and the more you practice using them in normal decision-making, the more quickly and even naturally they will guide you in a crisis—especially when things feel intense and confusing.

    In a crisis, the tendency is to justify abandoning values. However, assuming your core values are remotely ethical and actionable (sometimes value statements are so feel-good they don't make practical sense), they will function as a north star.

    Value statements shouldn't be left as a "feel-good" exercise. Options that help you express your values are probably good options. At a minimum, you shouldn't entertain options that violate your values.

Being clear about your principles or values helps with information because it is an immediate filter that you can use, appropriately reducing the options you are willing to explore to a few that are valuable to you.

As a clear example, let's say I lead an organization that is facing a financial crisis, and integrity is a value. Because of this value, I already know that fraudulent or deceptive behaviors aren't an option. As a result, I will immediately filter out any information that seems to drift in that direction.

This may seem obvious, but reflect on it a bit. How many leaders are you familiar with who claimed integrity as a value (everyone does), but then attempted to hide or spin the truth in a crisis? In most if not all of these instances, you'll probably also realize that their deceit eventually compounded or prolonged the problem.

b. **Vision.** Staying centered on your purpose or your why is critical. Along with principles, clarity of purpose (in the big and small picture) supports good decision-making.

Many decision-making conversations drift. They wander. They become driven by a strong personality or an urgency or a source of agitation. People can get confused or distracted by preferences in terms of methodology or approach—and forget about the ultimate purpose.

Purpose gets lost in a laundry list of to-dos. Stay centered on purpose.

During the "hunker down" periods of the COVID crisis, all of my clients who stayed focused on their purpose ended up having a record-breaking year. They adapted how they would accomplish their purpose, and they didn't get confused about what they were about.

c. **Priorities.** Not all decisions, strategies, or outcomes are equally important. When leaders have defined their priorities in advance, decision-making is easier. When those *priorities* are in alignment with your *values* and your *vision*, you build a way of quickly distinguishing good decisions from poor ones—in crisis or out.

Sometimes priorities need to change. But when change is intentional—as opposed to being reactive due to distraction or urgency—even the change process becomes an exercise of good judgment.

2. Evaluate objectively.

If you are clear about your principles, purpose, and priorities, it becomes easier to filter through the information that comes to you. Additionally, you know the information you need to seek.

Here are some questions that may help:

- Which options best align with our values?
- Which options move us toward (or the least distance away from) our vision?
- What do our top one to three priorities need to be? For example, if a family-owned enterprise is facing a crisis and may need to consider drastic changes, some priorities may remain consistent—for example, safety, respectful and transparent communication, and retention of core fixed assets.

A DECISION-MAKING PROCESS

These steps can help speed and focus your decision-making:

1. What are the primary issues facing us?

Think of issues as individual strings. In a crisis, they are often (not always) tangled together in a knotted ball. The mistake is to view the ball as a single issue. This creates confusion and conflict.

It helps, dramatically, to take a little time and identify and separate out individual issues from each other. It also helps to frame them as questions.

For example, imagine a crisis where a business has run out of cash and can't cover operational costs this coming month. Lines of credit are already maxed.

Individual issues, framed as questions, might include these:

- Without change, is this likely to be a short-term temporary problem or a chronic one?
- How do we cover payroll next month?
- How do we meet our contractual obligations?
- What internal or external factors and decisions led to this?

2. Recognize and then truth test assumptions.

A challenge in crisis is that we can start to assume certain things are true without having accurate data to support it. Many crises are grown because of reactions to inaccurate information.

These questions help:

- What do we actually know? What are we assuming or guessing at? This is difficult. Many assumptions are based on *some* accurate information.
- What are the primary sources of data? Go to the source. Talk to the people directly involved. Read the original documents.
- Can you verify the information? If you have questions about a source, seek at least two or three sources that can independently verify (or disprove) your information.
- Is this a one-off event that we think is becoming the new norm? It's easy in a crisis to jump to conclusions.

3. What is the most important or critical issue right now?

Crises can create a distorted sense of reality. The loudest voice or most urgent-looking need may not actually be the most important. Given your principles, purpose, and priorities, what is most important right now?

4. What can we control?
- Stopping or limiting damage
- Identifying anything we are doing or not doing that is contributing to the problem

- Identifying immediately available resources or help
- Ensuring we aren't exposing ourselves to more damage
- Getting help or assistance on the way

5. What can't we control?

- What is unfixable?
- What is beyond our ability or resources? (Do we control damage? Do we get help?)

6. Take action.

Good decisions only have value when put into action. Some leaders content themselves with a thorough decision-making process but then never follow through.

a. **Be decisive.** Out of fear of making a wrong or unpopular decision, too many leaders never make a decision at all. Instead, they keep putting decisions off until it's too late or something else forces a decision. This isn't wise, and it's poor leadership.

   I agree with the old saying "Haste makes waste." However, I've found that decent decisions *executed quickly* produce better results than perfect solutions *executed too slowly*. Aim for a B-quality decision—as in the letter grade. This means try to make a good decision. Don't worry about making the best decision.

b. **Adjust quickly.** During a crisis, speed is often important. Develop the habit of quick reflection. In the military, they call this "after-action reviews." They don't wait for the war to end to determine what is working and what needs to be improved. Leaders who build the habit of acting and reflecting grow. Leaders who don't reflect tend to repeat mistakes.

   An after-action review process is as simple as trying something, then making a point to ask questions like these:

- What happened?

- What did we intend to have happen?
- What accounts for the difference between what happened and what we intended?
- What can we learn from this?
- What will we do next?

COMMUNICATION IN CRISIS

How leaders communicate can either calm anxiety and unify efforts or compound the problems and divide your team.

Bruce T. Blythe, a respected leader in the crisis-management space identifies the following principles for relating to crisis:

1. Put the well-being of people first, with caring and compassion.
2. Assume appropriate responsibility for managing the crisis.
3. Address needs and concerns of all stakeholders in a timely manner.
4. Base all decisions and actions on honesty, legal guidelines, and ethical principles.
5. Maintain available, visible, and open communication with all affected parties.[53]

Notably, to communicate like this, you can't be in crisis mode yourself. In practical terms, it helps to develop a crisis communication plan to follow, which can be amended to fit specific situations as they become clearer.

Don't undervalue communication in crisis. Crises create a sense of uncertainty or fear. A lack of communication weakens trust. In the absence of trust, the choices of a leader are more likely to be interpreted as careless or malevolent.

Effective communication includes:

- **Stakeholder identification and engagement.** There may be several kinds or levels of stakeholders. Each may need a slightly different approach.
- **Facts and empathy.** People tend to divide into two camps around crises. Some have a high need to understand what is going on.

Others have a high need to be empathized with. Neither is right or wrong. Neither is better or worse. With groups, you'll need to communicate to both camps. Make sure your language and tone communicate empathy as well as providing adequate information.

Information should be accurate. The tendency is for some leaders to "massage the facts" for various reasons. If you do this, you can count on it undermining your credibility.

If you don't know something or can't share something, that should be communicated along with indicating when you'll come back with more information or what the next steps will be.

- **Frequency.** Determine the frequency with which you'll communicate. It is often best if this is scheduled. Consistency in when and how and even who delivers communication can contribute to a sense of structure and stability.

- **Credibility.** Credibility always matters but it is critical in a crisis, particularly a crisis that may be prolonged or that requires a big ask from stakeholders. If you haven't already built credibility, here are choices that will help:
  - Find someone in the community who is viewed as credible and trusted to deliver the message with you.
  - Consistently follow through on what you say you will do.
  - Be honest. If you lie, deliver half-truths, or engage in any kind of deception or manipulation of facts, it's likely to be found out and will undermine your credibility.
  - If you don't know something or don't have an answer, say so. But then let people know when they can expect to get an answer or update.
  - If possible and appropriate, let people know how they can help (themselves or others). Clear direction on helpful actions people can take will restore some sense of control.

Crises Are Make-or-Break Times for Leaders

During a crisis, some leaders are able to effectively rise to the occasion. Think of examples you are aware of: Likely they follow principles as I've described above. The leaders were prepared, but they also adapted. They were empathetic, but they also provided direction and acted. They communicated effectively.

Every choice they made may not have been the right or best one, but when they were in error, they quickly recognized it and adjusted. The totality of their decisions eventually led people through the crisis.

The principles in this chapter can help you do the same.

PUTTING IT INTO PRACTICE: EXERCISES

(These exercises are activities you can do before *you are in a crisis. The template above is designed to help you* during *a crisis.)*

- **Build your credibility "savings."** If you aren't sure if you currently have sufficient credibility to lead through a crisis, identify the top one or two actions you need to take to begin to improve it.
- **Prepare.** Identify one or two of the most likely crises you might face. Work through the preparation suggestions around them as detailed above.
- **Become decision-making experts.** Practice making good decisions faster. Make a habit of using your values and vision in this process. Pick a decision that is currently on your plate. Give yourself a limited amount of time, and practice making that decision within the time frame.
- **Practice consistent, clear, effective communication.** The principles for effective communication listed above apply—or can be easily adapted—to any situation.
  - Think through a recent, important communication. How well did it live up to these principles? What might be improved?
  - Think of an upcoming topic that needs to be communicated. How can you do so in a way that aligns with these principles?

ENDURANCE: STAYING WITH IT OVER THE LONG HAUL

*I do the very best I know how—the very best I can;
and I mean to keep on doing so until the end.* — Abraham Lincoln

Introduction to Endurance

R unning a marathon is hard. Or so I'm told. I've never ran one.

Many people run (or even walk) marathons. They persevere through months of training. They show up on race day. They complete the entire race, even if it takes them all day.

They don't quit. They feel great. (They should.) They post their very real accomplishment on social media. They frame their bib.

And then they stop running. Not just marathons—they stop running altogether.

This is a common occurrence in the sport and in leadership. People will persevere in a specific difficulty for a time or until a particular goal is hit—sometimes even significant goals and accomplishments. But once those have been accomplished, only some continue on.

STAYING HAPPY AND HEALTHY OVER THE LONG HAUL

I introduced the concept of *follow-through* earlier as a component of conditioning.

For our purposes, follow-through is the foundational ability to continue when success or reward seems elusive or doubtful. In my usage, it is the ability to overcome *internal resistance*: to keep driving yourself toward a goal regardless of frustrations, discouragements, setbacks, or failures. It is a basic mindset required for success.

"Endurance," as I'm defining it, includes follow-through, but it goes further to include an additional concept: the willingness to withstand or even voluntarily take on discomfort or even suffering in the intentional pursuit of long-term goals and then to do it again.

Follow-through is required to get into the game.

Endurance is required to stay in and excel over the long haul.

I understand this is splitting hairs to a certain degree. Maybe it's easiest to say endurance is what follow-through looks like when it grows up.

WHY THIS MATTERS

Simply put: Most likely, no one is depending on you to run a marathon. But people do depend on your leadership. If a runner quits midrace or decides to just have a one-and-done race, it primarily matters only to them.

However, if a leader quits prematurely—especially if they quit leading without appropriately handing over the position of leadership—it influences other people. And leaders do this. They get tired, discouraged, or distracted. Some walk away from positions or opportunities. Others quit while on the job. They come to work, move things around on their desk, and handle basic management issues, but they stop leading.

In any endeavor that requires endurance, all of the reasons to quit will eventually emerge. Even when you are finally successful, they'll show up: you've tried hard enough and done more than others, you've proven your point, or no one should be expected to deal with X, Y, or Z for this long.

CHARACTERISTICS OF ENDURANCE

Leaders who've been successful in their roles over the long haul do these four things:

- **Consistently follow through.** I mentioned this earlier, but to recap: It's easy to plan, but it is difficult to implement. Many leaders love to dream and scheme. They get bored or distracted from the follow-through. High-endurance leaders know how to see something through to the end.

- **Set up systems and structures.** High-endurance leaders appreciate and respect the nonsexy side of organizations. They recognize the need to stop reinventing the wheel. They set up systems and structures so that consistent results can be achieved by more people with less effort. Make endurance easy.

- **Create accountability.** High-endurance leaders learn that it's easier to go further if you aren't working as hard. They know they don't have to work as hard when everyone on their team (including themselves) will reliably do what they said they would do in the timing and at the quality required. These leaders transparently set goals, monitor progress, have tough conversations, and adjust as needed.

- **Renew vision.** Leaders need to renew and reconnect to their personal and organizational vision periodically. High-endurance leaders know how to do this and take time for it. They also accept that most people get distracted and forget. Very few people have the responsibility to constantly think about the big picture. As a result, the immediate and short-term can easily capture most people's attention. This is why effective leaders constantly refer to values, vision, purpose, and passion through the whole organization. .

We'll explore each of these in the following chapters.

CHAPTER 22

Perseverance: Sustain Success

I recently had the opportunity to take my family to Nome, Alaska, to watch the finish of the Iditarod. If you aren't familiar with it, the Iditarod is a long-distance dogsled race across Alaska. By long-distance, we're talking 1,000 miles give or take, depending on how the race is routed each year.

The race itself commemorates a heroic effort in 1925 to save lives. At that time, there was a diphtheria epidemic in Nome. After an urgent search, a supply of diphtheria antitoxin was discovered. But it was in Anchorage, 1,000 miles away.[54]

Back then, airplanes weren't able to make the flight, and ships were too slow. But dog teams were able to make it happen. A complex effort was launched to get the antitoxin to Nome as quickly as possible. The nation's attention was captured. The press christened it "The Great Race of Mercy."[55]

Now, it's an annual race that takes between eight and 15 days to complete. Not everyone who starts finishes. You aren't even allowed to start unless you have a number of long-distance races under your belt. Additionally, you need an experienced Iditarod finisher to vouch for you: someone who believes you have the right stuff.

Racing for up to two weeks, mostly alone, in the Arctic winter isn't for beginners or quitters. It's for tough people who've already proven themselves. And the only way you prove yourself in extreme endurance events is to keep getting up and doing what needs to be done—again and again. Follow through.

The winners become local heroes. But even the Red Lantern winner (the last-place finisher) earns respect.[56] They finished. Just finishing is an accomplishment few others can match.

The ability to persevere over the long haul—not everyone has it.

ENDURANCE AND CREDIBILITY

Long-term endurance for leaders is about consistent perseverance and follow-through over time. This consistency, this reliability, builds credibility.

Credibility is the currency of leadership. The more credibility a leader has, the more likely others will support or follow. Credibility takes time to build, and if it is damaged, it takes time to rebuild.

It's simple. The more you lead well, the easier it becomes to lead well. Like compound interest, the longer you keep following through on what you say and promise, the more people are likely to look to and defer to your leadership.

As simple as it sounds, not many are willing to do what it takes to start leading well. And even fewer keep at it—consistently—over time.

Leaders are responsible to others and for themselves.

Every leader, ultimately, has only one person they can actually control. Themself.

But many leaders find that they struggle with leading and managing themselves. They struggle with directing and sustaining personal growth. And they struggle with managing their basic habits, emotions, and behaviors.

This is why I often say that leadership development is personal development. As a leader allows themself to grow and mature, so does their ability to lead. But this takes effort, not just time.

When the leader stops actively growing or maturing, they don't just coast. They begin to atrophy as people. If they stop growing, they begin their decline.

For experienced leaders who've earned respect and success, there can be an understandable tendency to want to take their foot off the gas. They have learned a lot. They have done a lot. They know a lot. But having done something in the past isn't the same thing as getting up and doing it again today or tomorrow.

If we stay in leadership, we continue to have a responsibility to others. Our ability to meet that responsibility is dependent on how we responsible we remain for ourselves.

SUCCESS HABITS

A very small key that opens the door to big success over the long haul is *success habits*: small, simple, sometimes mundane behaviors that, over time, aggregate into big success. These are often the recommended practices discussed earlier in the section on Healthy Habits and Conditioning.

The practices that I introduced earlier in this book are the kinds of habits that create and support long-term success. All of them need to be maintained, like fitness habits or hygiene habits. You can't bank the number of steps you took each day or donuts you avoided or teeth that you brushed.

PUTTING IT INTO PRACTICE: EXERCISES

What practices, relationships, or projects do you need to commit to persevere all of the way on? What help do you need to do it?

Accountability: Everyone Does What They Say They Will Do

Any coach or fitness trainer will tell you that providing accountability is a major part of their role. It doesn't matter who they are working with.

Anyone can download a fitness or nutrition plan, but it helps to have someone spot your form when you are tired. Or challenge you when you fall into a rut. Or keep you consistent when you don't feel like working out.

While it is always valuable to have a coach, as you grow you learn to keep yourself accountable as well. An acquaintance was a competitive swimmer while in elementary school. Since his school didn't have enough swim coaches, he was handed a workout that he needed to complete on his own. As a child, he had to learn to make himself do things.

As leaders grow, age, and mature, external sources of accountability become scarcer. It's important to find them and build them in. But it's also valuable to learn to keep yourself accountable. Last, it's important to keep your team accountable.

"BEFORE" PICTURES OF ACCOUNTABILITY

A CEO feels as if she never has time to really focus on what is important. She works long hours and is proud of this, but she feels as if she is always playing catch-up. She also allows a constant flow of interruptions throughout her day. It's rare that she has 30 minutes of uninterrupted time together to concentrate.

An owner is struggling in his business and doesn't understand why. Revenues are high, but there is never any money. He often needs to forgo paying himself to cover payroll. As a small business, the bookkeeping is minimal with informal financial management. He was frustrated to find that a longtime employee had been embezzling from him—he's not even sure for how much. He'd like to sell his company, but buyers always ask for his financial statements. His books aren't current, and he's never able to respond.

A supervisor is stressed by employees who frequently show up late to work. Their presence is necessary for others to do their work. So, 15 minutes of tardiness pushes an entire team back in their schedule. This happens several times a week. She is frustrated and doesn't know what to do.

Accountability, done well, protects and benefits others.

Accountability protects the investment of time, effort, and skill that your team puts into accomplishing projects. It protects resources. It allows for margin and predictability. It creates and supports healthy boundaries.

Why let that be robbed?

Many leaders struggle with or even resist building cultures of accountability. As a result, they spend an enormous amount of time, energy, and resources chasing after their tails. This is usually for four reasons:

1. **They want to be liked.** Most leaders don't want to be the stereotypical mean boss. They don't want to confront. They don't want to say "no" or "not now" or "hurry up." They are afraid that if they hold others to account, they'll be viewed as that mean boss.

2. **It takes work.** To create a culture of accountability requires leaders to take time to clearly define their expectations. Many leaders find this difficult. It takes less effort to have fuzzy goals with vaguely communicated expectations. This creates the perception

of direction without having to do any heavy lifting.

3. **They view accountability as conflict and conflict as wrong.** Similar to wanting to be liked, many leaders view checking in on progress as a confrontation, or a conflict. They are uncomfortable with this because it feels wrong. So, they try to avoid it.

4. **They don't want to be accountable themselves.** Many leaders don't particularly want to be accountable for their own actions or decisions. Why be the boss if you have to report to others? Or be disciplined? Like it or not, their own lack of accountability defines the values and culture that model the way others follow.

ACCOUNTABLE FOR WHAT?

One reason people don't like accountability is that they've often experienced being held to account for insignificant things while what's important slips by. That's frustrating.

Address this by structuring accountability practices in your organizational values and the results (or outcomes) that you are pursuing. This is the why that people like to talk about. Your values and your purpose should orient and inform accountability. Specifically, there should be accountability in these three areas:

1. **Ethics.** Teach or define what is expected in terms of ethical behavior. Don't tolerate or excuse a lack of ethics. You can teach skills: It's very hard to teach character. Act ethically (model it) and expect the same from your team.

2. **Attitude.** One person's poor attitude is rarely contained to one person. It's felt by and affects other employees, customers, and partners. Granted, attitude is fuzzy and not always easy to define. However, the impact of poor attitude has hard numbers: a weak bottom line, turnover, hours spent in conflict, lost customers, or goals left incomplete.

3. **Performance.** The clearer you are about what good performance looks like, the easier it is for others to get there. The clearer you

are, the easier it is to measure (for yourself and for your employees). Clarity supports high performance. It also makes it easier for you to diagnose and address issues that are preventing high performance.

FIVE TIPS FOR BUILDING A CULTURE OF ACCOUNTABILITY

To create or reshape culture, you need to evaluate your own values or world view around accountability. If you aren't personally accountable in some real and tangible way, you will struggle to make accountability part of your organizational culture.

1. Pay attention to your own responses to accountability.

Accountability starts at the top. As a leader, the more you allow yourself (your ethics, attitude, and performance) to be meaningfully held to account, the more naturally everyone else will as well.

A lack of accountability within a team or organization is nearly always indicative of a lack of accountability on the part of leadership. This is so predictable that when conducting organizational assessments, I can learn an enormous amount about the leaders of an organization—without even meeting them—by observing the practices of several of their frontline teams.

2. Accountability should be focused on values and purpose.

Major on the majors, and minor on the minors. Make sure you know which is which. Shape accountability to be in alignment with your stated values and purpose (goals or outcomes) for your organization. Those are majors.

Don't get distracted by small acts and minor issues. If the time someone shows up for work doesn't affect anyone else, violate your organizational values, or detract from accomplishing your purpose, then it really doesn't matter much. But if showing up late negatively affects others, violates your values, or makes it harder to accomplish your purpose, then it matters a great deal. Deal with it appropriately.

3. Get comfortable with forthrightness.

Forthrightness means to be unambiguous, direct, straightforward, honest.

I'm not a huge fan of beating around the bush or avoiding issues. People usually act that way out of a desire to avoid conflict, but it often ends up hurting people.

It's an important leadership characteristic to be forthright. To do this it's important to understand how others feel respected. It's also important to leave room for others to provide their perspective. Some leaders forget about power dynamics and how their opinion (or stray thought) can feel like a directive to others. My book *Conflict and Leadership* provides a practical guide—and even scripts—to help you learn how to be forthright effectively.

4. Clarify expectations with clear indicators of success/metrics.

One of the biggest challenges around accountability is that we never actually put a sharp point on what success looks like. Many executives and owners tell me, "I'll just know it when things are running right."

Fine. Maybe you will. But no one else around you will. They won't know what you expect. They won't be able to measure progress or the lack thereof. Truth be told, neither will you.

I always push back when given that answer. One reason I ask this question with a client before accepting an engagement is that I know my services will be evaluated. I want it to be explicitly clear on *how*. I have no interest in leaving the interpretation of my success vulnerable to someone's bad day.

The other reason is, I want crystal clarity on what I'm working toward. Over time, on a long project, it can be easy for focus to wander. Clarity in expectations brings us all back.

5. Plan your check-ins.

Schedule check-ins regularly. The frequency and length should match the need. I recommend keeping things as short as possible. But at the beginning, meet more frequently and back off as seems appropriate.

A planned check-in accomplishes at least four things:

It creates a coaching or mentoring opportunity. More frequent, highly focused check-in conversations allow you to grow someone in real time. This is enormously valuable, and most employees want it. It is a dramatically more valuable practice than the annual review that everyone hates.

It makes sure the conversations happen. For the most part, these kinds of conversations tend not to happen unless they are scheduled. The can is kicked down the road. Either everyone forgets what was agreed on, or the discussion waits until frustration on someone's part forces a (less effective) conversation.

It depersonalizes accountability. With clear metrics and scheduled times to report, the personal element of accountability is largely taken out. Don't let the only time you talk about progress be when you are frustrated about something.

It takes the fear out of accountability. Accountability is just checking in. It's just a conversation, but for many people, it feels like a confrontation. That triggers all kinds of emotions—often fear. As a result of fear, people avoid the conversation until they are frustrated or angry enough to have it. Not helpful.

Also, most employees indicate wanting to know about their progress and how leaders feel the employees are doing. Generally, employees will say they don't have all the feedback they want. Planning these conversations makes it just part of the routine. It's not like being called to the principal's office.

"AFTER" PICTURES OF ACCOUNTABILITY

The CEO has clearly defined what her team needs to accomplish and by when. Clarity has made her team more focused and effective. Her meetings with them now take a fraction of the time they used to. Her company's performance has taken off, and she works less. She is rarely at work after five, and her weekends are for her family and personal rejuvenation.

The owner hired a consultant to help him build a financial management system and to teach him how to use financial information to manage the company. Armed with that knowledge, he's moved the company from having lower margins than the industry norm to being consistently higher. He recently received an unexpected offer to sell his company. This time he was delighted to find that he was ready to present his financials and knew how to use them confidently to negotiate.

The supervisor enjoys going to work with her smoothly running team. Employees are rarely ever late now. Everyone is able to hit goals without work spilling over to the next day. She had simply announced to the team that timeliness was going to be a requirement moving forward. She explained how tardiness affected everyone else, and she reintroduced everyone to an existing policy on timeliness. She followed this up with private conversations with the offending employees. She let them know they were valued but needed to be on time and that she would enforce it. To her surprise, there was no pushback. They knew they were out of line and just needed the nudge.

BEGIN WITH YOURSELF: CREATE A STRUCTURE FOR OTHERS

You will only build organizational accountability if you personally value it and make it an active part of your own life. To be truly accountable, we need to answer to someone else. If accountability isn't part of your leadership structure, you need to intentionally build it in.

PUTTING IT INTO PRACTICE: EXERCISES

Ensure that in all of your meetings you assign actions.
Who is responsible?
What are they responsible for?
How will we know they've made progress?
When is this due?

- Build your own accountability. This needs to be to someone (or several people) you don't want to disappoint. This could be your team, a spouse, members of a mastermind or peer-mentoring group, or a coach. It's important that you respect them and want their respect.

- Let them know what you are trying to accomplish.
- Make it easy for them to evaluate your progress, or commit to sharing progress with them.
- Set deadlines for yourself. Plan to report back on those deadlines.

CHAPTER 24

Structure and Systems: Putting Great Leadership on Autopilot

LEADERS CAN GO FARTHER, LONGER WITH STRUCTURES AND SYSTEMS

As a teenager in the 1930s, Carlos Gracie started developing the techniques that would evolve into Brazilian jiu-jitsu. At the time, his brother Helio was sickly. His doctor originally wouldn't allow him to train, but when Helio turned 16, though he was still weak and small, he began to train with Carlos.[57]

Helio remained small and weak his entire life. Though he was fascinated by martial arts, he realized that many of the techniques he was learning benefited from strength and size. In his own words: "I could not manage to do what my brother [Carlos] did, because his jiu-jitsu depended on strength and ability. I had neither the one nor the other of those. Then I made that which is known today. I perfected the flawed technique of my brother on behalf of weaker people, using the principles of physics, like force and the leverage."[58]

He adapted what he was learning so that the smaller and weaker opponent could defeat (or at least neutralize) the bigger and stronger opponent. He successfully fought and competed for over 30 years in part to prove the efficacy of BJJ.

Helio died when he was 95 years old. He continued to train on the mats right up until the week before he died. He'd learned the secret to longevity, especially athletic longevity. And it wasn't about trying harder.[59]

SMARTER, NOT HARDER

To the uninitiated, a BJJ match can often look confusing. At times it is dynamic. At times it appears nothing is happening.

But practitioners see the structures of body mechanics in a fight. In BJJ, we often use terms like "frames," "levers," and "space." We talk about alignment and positioning.

BJJ—like all martial arts—is a *system* of principles and precise movements. It is consistent. It can be repeated, demonstrated, and taught. You can troubleshoot it.

Systems are like recipes. They describe how to move from one position, or *structure,* to another: How do get your grips on an opponent? How do you take them to the ground? How do you establish a dominant position? How do you escape a weak position? How do you set up a submission?

POSITION BEFORE SUBMISSION

A very common phrase in BJJ is "position before submission." This means using *systems* to establish the right *structures* before you attempt to submit your opponent. If you have a strong position, a submission is much easier. The ability to do this is what is referred to as "technique."

Technique is difficult for beginners to learn—more so if they are athletic and strong. They often want to jump right into manhandling an opponent. I was guilty of this when I started, and I was shocked to find myself being tossed around, seemingly without effort, by people smaller than myself.

Technique, particularly the ability to recognize what structures are needed and the systems to move between them, is what will allow you to lead sustained success.

THE IMPORTANCE OF BUILDING SIMPLE AND CONSISTENT SYSTEMS AND STRUCTURES

I often work with clients who hope to scale, find freedom from the day-to-day, or who want to exit their business. They are often already successful, but they achieved it by brute force. They've hustled their way into success. They will quickly describe the long hours, heavy travel, and late nights.

That approach is exhausting. A sense of overwhelm grows as a business becomes more complicated, as the risks seem heavier, or as the number of moving parts grows and moves faster.

At a certain point, these leaders can't keep up. It's too complicated, or they are too tired to maintain—let alone increase—forward momentum. They may not quit, but they start to ride the brake.

The solution is to build the systems and structures that allow optimal, predictable results that others can follow with minimal effort.

While this takes up-front investment or effort, it dramatically reduces the ongoing effort the leader (or anyone else) needs to make. It's using technique instead of brute force.

The better a company sets up their systems and structures, the bigger they can grow, the more freedom the leader has, and the more valuable (and easier to sell) the company becomes.

WHAT SYSTEMS AND STRUCTURES CAN DO FOR YOU

Consider the value difference between two restaurants—a McDonald's (or any franchise) vs. the local favorite burger pub.

At the time that I'm writing, if you want to buy an existing McDonald's franchise, expect to pay at least U.S. $1 million. It could easily be higher. (This excludes real estate costs. McDonald's typically owns 40% of a franchise's land and 70% of the building.)

Compare this to the burger pub down the street. It probably offers a superior product and a nicer customer experience. But in most cases, it'll never find a buyer. Excluding the liquidation value of real estate and chipped cups, the business value is $0. For this reason, many business brokers and mergers and acquisitions advisers won't even offer to sell restaurants.

Why?

SYSTEMS AND STRUCTURES

McDonald's offers franchisees a "business in a box." They are selling the recipe for success. They understand what it takes for the business to work. They understand the structures that both represent the brand and that achieve operational efficiencies. They've codified the systems that create reliable, predictable results.

Your local burger pub rarely has any of this. The outgoing owner is often the chief cook and bottle washer. Also, they do all the buying, hiring, kitchen, and the front-of-house management, financial management, and marketing. Usually, their recipe for success is hidden away in their mind, which they can't sell.

Structures and systems are the difference between a restaurant that has value and one that doesn't. They are the difference between one where the owner isn't involved in the day-to-day and one where the owner is lucky to get away for a vacation at all.

That being said, the burger pub owner doesn't need to resign himself to this fate. He could identify and capture the systems and structures. He could write out his recipe for success. The owners who do this are (often) the ones who go on to expand to multiple locations or open new restaurant concepts.

At this point, they graduate from being chief cook and bottle washer. Now they are a restaurateur, or they found a new franchise. That is valuable. *And at that point, even though the business is larger and more complex, they usually aren't working as hard as the chief cook and bottle washer!*

WHAT SYSTEMS AND STRUCTURES LOOK LIKE

There are various systems and structures that an organization can put in place to improve its overall efficiency and effectiveness. Consider these examples:

Standard operating procedures (SOPs). These are documented procedures that outline the steps required to complete a specific task or process. SOPs help ensure consistency and efficiency in how tasks are performed, and they also provide a reference point for employees.

Organizational charts. These diagrams depict the structure of an organization, including the roles and responsibilities of each employee or department. Organizational charts help employees understand where they fit in the larger organization and who they report to.

Performance-management systems. These systems help managers track employee performance, set goals, and provide feedback. Performance-management systems can include regular check-ins, goal-setting processes, and annual performance reviews.

Communication systems. Effective communication is essential in any organization. Communication systems can include regular team meetings, email protocols, and collaboration tools, like instant messaging and project management software.

Quality control systems. Quality control systems are designed to ensure that products or services meet a certain standard of quality. These systems can include testing and inspection procedures, quality audits, and customer feedback mechanisms.

Financial management systems. These systems help organizations manage their finances, including budgeting, forecasting, and financial reporting.

Building layout. Optimizing the use of space creates efficiency, improves safety, and supports consistency. Physical layouts of bars, auto-service garages, or offices can strengthen communication, improve customer satisfaction (even if they never see it), increase productivity, lower operational costs, and add to the bottom line.

Overall, these systems and structures help organizations be more efficient, improve productivity, strengthen communication, reduce errors and mistakes, and improve the satisfaction of both employees and customers.

It's a win, win, win, win, win, win.

IMPLEMENTING SIMPLE AND CONSISTENT SYSTEMS AND STRUCTURES

"Where do we start?" Many leaders or teams feel overwhelmed by this.

First of all, some things shouldn't be a do-it-yourself project. An HR consultant, a fractional CFO, or a process-improvement professional can help you accomplish in weeks or months what might take you years on your own.

It's brute force to trade time for money. It's technique to use money to buy time. You and your team already have full-time jobs.

However, there are times when do-it-yourself makes better sense, or leaders will insist on it regardless. In those instances, follow this process:

1. Create a small team (even just two people) who will spearhead this effort. Create a regular meeting schedule. Stay accountable to forward movement.

2. Write a master list of the major systems and structures that need to be improved or defined. This should be a brain dump exercise. It doesn't need to be exhaustive. Don't get stuck on trying to think of everything. Get out a clock and set it for 10 minutes. List as much as you can.

3. Review the list and identify items that are the most critical to your organization.
   - When developed, which ones will create the greatest benefit?
   - If not developed, which ones expose you to the greatest risk?

4. Of those, which are the easiest to pursue? (This is at the beginning. Tackle larger ones as you become more comfortable with the process.)

5. If you've identified a large system or a system of systems (for example, hiring), break it down into its major components (advertising, recruiting, applications, screening, onboarding).

6. Set aside time to regularly record how-tos. Often a simple outline does this sufficiently well. Some people use videos to capture how they do things. Aim for just enough information.

7. Accept a B-grade effort. It can always be improved later. For now, do a solid, good-enough job.

8. For documents or systems, make sure they are filed in a common, accessible place with an easy-to-use filing system.

9. Introduce the system or structure to all the users. Explain why and the value it will bring.

10. Enforce the use of it and keep people accountable.

11. Improve it as you go, as people use it, and as you learn its strengths and weaknesses.

VISION, VALUES, STRUCTURES, AND SYSTEMS

One of the most common areas of resistance to building systems and structures comes from people who like the informal, warm family feel of an organization. They don't want their workplace to feel corporate or bureaucratic.

I get it. That's the right gut instinct. The problem is that informality will not support growth. Also, it often primarily benefits the old-timers or the inner circle. And, truth be told, "family" in a business isn't a true family. Real families are unconditionally family. In business—even a family-feeling business—there will be expectations (even if ambiguously defined) that have to be met to be part of the family.

Here's how to navigate this:

- Stay true and aligned to your values and vision.
- Remember that structures (like those from accounting, HR, sales, etc.) serve the values and vision, not the other way around. Never let the tail wag the dog.

- Any new system or structure should be designed with two goals in mind:
    - *Ideally*, it should protect or manifest one or more of your values as well as move you toward your vision.
    - *Minimally*, it should never compromise a value or create friction on the path toward your vision.

- Don't be *reactive*.
    - Don't create a new system or structure just because it's what all the cool kids are doing. There is always some new policy scare or fad out there. Be led by your vision and values, not headlines.
    - Be careful when changing a system or structure because of a recent workplace catastrophe or embarrassment. The problem may have identified an area where work needs to be done, but make sure that what you develop serves your overall values and vision. Don't just cut and paste someone else's language. (I can see the "scars" of past scandals all over some organizations' policies or bylaws. Because they are reactive and poorly thought through, they tend to move the organization toward inaction as opposed to effective or healthy action. They may even directly conflict with your core values and vision.)

PUTTING IT INTO PRACTICE: EXERCISES

- Make a brain dump master list of all the key systems and structures you can think of.
- Identify which will be better served by bringing in a professional adviser to help.
- Identify which you will build internally. Create your team, pick one or a few to work on, and execute.

Renew Vision: Vision Needs to Stay Fresh

Remember chapter 16, "Encourage the Heart"? Renewing vision is similar. But this is something you need to do for yourself.

One winter, some friends and I tracked two caribou deep into a valley on a remote Aleutian island. On the farthest reach of the valley, we came across a small herd. There were four of us, and we took eight caribou.

It was late in the afternoon. By the time we had finished field dressing, it was dark. We decided the best thing to do was to cache the meat and come back for it the next day. We hadn't planned to be out overnight.

The valley was treeless. In daylight, it was easy to pick a path through the snow-filled ravines, cliffs, and creek beds. Getting lost was impossible. Maps and GPS were unnecessary. Everything was visible. In the dark, as the temperature dropped, I looked at the night sky and took my bearings from the stars. But soon, clouds rolled in, and my view of the night sky was lost.

There was nothing else to do. We began to hike out.

The clouds brought heavy snow and wind. Our vision was limited to only about 10 feet. Our trail was erased. We had no path to follow. The terrain had suddenly become a labyrinth without lights.

I was breaking trail, navigating for all of us. Even if we'd had maps or GPS, it wouldn't have indicated the relatively small but still Impassable cliffs and ravines that snaked over the valley. We had regularly forced detours, but it was impossible to discern which way to detour.

Due to the nature of the terrain, it was often easiest to keep moving higher up the southern mountain range—but easiest doesn't mean easy. We also knew we would need to descend and cross the valley to the north at some point to get out, so we didn't want to climb too high.

I began to hear the discouragement and exhaustion in my friends' voices.

One, either from overexertion or illness, fell a couple of times. He began to puke.

"Just go on," he said.

We got him back to his feet. But he was struggling.

Our energy was depleted. We were cold. We couldn't see which way to go.

One of my hunting companions had brought his teenage son. They were walking directly behind me. I overheard the son say, "Dad, are we going to make it out of here?"

It was a nightmare.

Vision Can Fade or Be Confused

It seems obvious that you need to get out of a situation like that. But exhaustion and emotion can obscure judgment. Foolish rationalizations suddenly appear prescient. "Let's stop. We'll just sit for a while. Maybe we can ride this storm out."

This is how people die.

As anyone who has participated in endurance sports knows, one of the biggest challenges you face is yourself. You are alone with your thoughts for extended periods of time. Discomfort, boredom, fatigue, pain, or fear can overwhelm perspective. It's very easy to think, "You know, I've gone far enough." There are a million reasons to justify it. Any one of them can seem good enough.

It's easy to lose hope or sense of your goal. It's one thing to inspire someone to undertake a long, difficult task or journey. It's another thing to renew that inspiration to complete it.

When we began hiking out, I was just one member of the hunting party. But by breaking trail, I had assumed a kind of leadership without thinking about it.

I realized that my friends were not only following my trail but also my level of hope and confidence. I needed to maintain a positive vision that we would all get out safely, and I needed to help sustain this vision in everyone else. The potential consequences were too high if anyone lost hope or stopped.

VISION CAN BE LOST: LEADERS HAVE TO RENEW IT

Vision. The answer to "Why am I doing this?" can be lost, and it needs to be recovered. Renewed. For yourself and those you lead.

A core leadership strength is the ability to *inspire a shared vision*. Frankly, inspiring a shared vision is often not that difficult once you know how.

However, *renewing* a personal sense of vision when you are bored, distracted, tired, discouraged, or overwhelmed is something else. Being able to renew everyone else's sense of vision is yet another thing altogether.

I couldn't just tell my wife "I love you" on our wedding day and call it good. I need to communicate "I love you" through my words and actions on an ongoing basis.

Similarly, our teams need their vision consistently renewed. It isn't enough to touch on it once a planning cycle. It should be part of our regular conversations, even on a daily basis.

Leaders often have the luxury (though frequently unused) to set, think about, and adjust their vision as they go. But many—possibly most—people on your team don't. Their responsibilities are necessarily more focused and often shorter term in range. They routinely deal with accomplishing immediate tasks and solving problems.

They get tired, overwhelmed, or distracted. It can be easy for them to lose sight of the big picture or to forget about their why.

HOW TO RENEW VISION

If you followed my recommendations earlier in the book, your team was involved in developing the original vision. This makes renewing their vision not just easier but possible. If you didn't, you'll be stuck trying to renew a vision they never had. That won't work and will just frustrate or confuse everyone involved. Here are three tips for renewing vision:

1. **Remind yourself regularly.** Leaders are often busy and don't make time for reflection. Being busy can cloud a sense of vision. To address this, leaders should make it a habit to regularly take time alone to reconnect with their vision.

   I recommend writing down your vision. Then read it to yourself on a daily basis. My normal practice is to read mine when I wake up. It helps me quickly regain my bearings for the day.

2. **Remind your team regularly.** I heard one leader say, "Teams leak." They leak vision. They forget. They get distracted. They need to have their "vision levels" regularly checked and refilled. Your team needs to be reminded both of the vision and of their progress. Chances are high that they forgot the first and can't see the latter.

   When leaders communicate to their teams, they should refer to the vision constantly. This should be both planned and spontaneous: through extravagant retreats as well as daily reminders. You cannot refer to it too much.

3. **Vision is better with a friend.** Being around other people who are actively pursuing their clear, inspiring vision will reenergize your own, even if their vision is different from yours. Find these people. Seek them out. Go to meetings or conferences where they

are. Build relationships and friendships with them. Their new (to you) energies, perspectives, observations, and responses to challenges will reinspire you.

Be careful to curate who you spend your time around. Ensure that you are with people who are producing results and making tangible progress toward their vision.

Don't spend time with pretend leaders who don't take action. Their negative energy is *also* infectious. Get away from it.

RENEWING VISION

As I broke trail, in the darkness, through the snow, I needed to maintain my own sense of direction, both in the vision that we would be successful and in finding navigation points that would help guide us. That night, my friends needed me to find the direction and confidence for them.

I have had plenty of other experiences where I've needed this from others. In this instance, I couldn't surround myself with encouragers, but as I trudged through the snow, I remembered past encouragers from all of the many hunting and mountaineering stories I heard growing up and the survival trainings I'd been through. I took encouragement and guidance from them.

It was a long night. But we made it out. And we did it by forcing ourselves to see the outcome we wanted when it was no longer visible.

PUTTING IT INTO PRACTICE: EXERCISES

- Remind yourself of your vision:
  - Write out your vision. Make a list of why accomplishing it matters. Add what the consequences are for not accomplishing it.
  - For 21 days, make a practice of reading your vision and your whys.
  - If you find that helpful, make it an ongoing practice.

- Remind others of the vision:
    - Find a way to reference organizational vision one time each day. Do this for 21 days.
    - Explore with your team how they will benefit from the vision and what they'll lose or miss out on if it isn't accomplished. (They need their own why. Yours may not motivate them.)
    - Clarify how a goal moves everyone toward the vision.
    - Explain how an accomplishment supports the vision.

CHAPTER 26

Self-Maintenance and Recovery: The Key to Longevity and Growth

Want better results over time? Put in more effort.

Well ... that isn't how things actually work.

Consider athletes. Your average athlete would prefer to train harder rather than do mobility drills, sit in an ice bath, take a break, or make sure they get enough sleep. But the body can only train so much, then it plateaus or breaks down. In most cases, training is the stimulus for growth (physical adaptations). But that growth happens during times of recovery.

Recovering well is a discipline and a skill. However, like athletes, many leaders equate more effort with more results. Plus, they just love the game. It's hard to know when and how to back off.

I'd like to introduce four key athletic concepts of recovery—mobility, stretching, rest, and healing—and how leaders can incorporate these concepts into their leadership practices.

MOBILITY

Mobility is the ability to move a joint freely and easily—through a *full range of motion*—without discomfort or pain.

In leadership, how well or easily do you move through your full range of motion? Are there leadership behaviors or priorities that feel limited to you? Or rough? Or painful? For example, how comfortable are you with fully engaging in the core leadership strengths:

- Inspiring a shared sense of vision
- Encouraging the members of your team
- Enabling others to act
- Being a role model to others
- Challenging processes or behaviors when needed

Is there one or more of these that don't feel as comfortable for you as the others? Perhaps you feel there is a limitation or block of some kind. It's worthwhile to take a periodic scan and explore your current limits and options for expanding your mobility.

STRETCHING

Stretching is a process where we teach a muscle or muscle group to un-clench and let go. Muscles are tight because our body believes that a particular movement is unsafe. This may be due to underuse, overuse, or injury. The muscle tightens to limit movement and prevent damage. This is a helpful risk-mitigation default setting for our bodies, but our bodies aren't always right.

We do this as leaders. There are habits, challenges, and practices that—due to underuse, overuse, or an injury of some sort—we (or our teams) perceive as unsafe. Here are some examples:

- Entrepreneurs start out with high-risk tolerances, then achieve success and stop taking risks.

- Policies become over-restrictive because of a damaging or embarrassing incident in the past.
- Appropriate confrontation and candor are avoided.
- Unfamiliar, but helpful, workplace practices or habits are tried and then discarded because they feel uncomfortable.
- Leaders micromanage because they don't know how to build systems of trust.

It's important to pay attention to places where you or your team seem tight. In most cases, tightness should signal a need to work on that area, not to avoid it.

REST

Athletes who are following a well-designed program will frequently rest. They will rest between sets and after a training. They'll build in longer periods of rest on regular cycles (often somewhere between eight and 12 weeks of heavy training). They will prioritize sleep.

Physically stressing the body triggers the central nervous system to adapt and grow. But that growth occurs while you rest—primarily when you sleep—not while you work out.

Rest is crucial for leaders and is taken in ways that are similar to those of athletes:

- Taking frequent breaks during the day
- Knowing when you've worked enough for the day and stopping
- Sleeping well at night
- Taking periodic breaks away from work—vacations, sabbaticals, etc.
- Cross-training with something "light," such as attending a conference, connecting with peers, or participating in team retreats

Burnout and chronic stress lead to physical and mental health issues. This ultimately affects team performance and morale. By prioritizing rest, leaders can help prevent burnout and ensure that they and their team are able to perform at their best.

HEALING

As I write, I'm recovering from a dislocated finger. This occurred while practicing BJJ. I removed the top half of my finger from the bottom. The doctor put them back together, but my finger needs to heal. All of the sports I practice require using my hands. I've been forced to the sidelines, and it is awful.

Healing refers to the process of recovering from physical or emotional injuries, such as muscle strains or emotional stress. Athletes *hate* stopping to heal, and as a result, many prolong their injuries or make them permanent. Others are so afraid of getting hurt that they don't see healing as something normal.

BJJ scores relatively high in terms of "macho culture." Injuries are common and can be seen as badges of honor. It's important for a gym to cultivate a culture that allows and encourages people to stop and heal. Otherwise, no one will recover, and everyone will be perpetually wounded or will quit—kind of like a lot of workplaces.

In fact, recovering from injuries has sparked some of my greatest growth in BJJ. Injuries increase my awareness and force me to try things I previously avoided or never considered. As much as I hate being injured, I've learned that injury can be an opportunity.

As a leader, it is important to create a supportive environment that promotes healing. As the saying goes, "Hurt people hurt people." Life can bang people up. Our jobs can take a toll. It's important to model the ability to recognize when you may be injured. It can include providing resources such as coaching, employee assistance programs, health benefits, and flexible work arrangements.

The danger with healing is that instead of focusing on recovery, doing our physical therapy, and building new strength, we cultivate and even encourage weakness.

True healing is a restoration of strength and ability; it isn't primarily about the cessation of discomfort. Like a lot of physical therapy, a healing process may not be comfortable. It takes toughness to heal well. Healing well is different from having "safe rooms" in your office and coloring books for your adults. Those nurture and normalize weakness and injury.

A healing culture is one where leaders are clear eyed about injuries and make a priority about restoring themselves and their teams to full operating capacity.

VALUING RECOVERY AS LEADERS

Incorporate these concepts of mobility, stretching, rest, and healing into your leadership. They will help you lead more effectively over the long haul. They'll protect you and your team from burnout, unforced errors, and diminished returns.

Promote a robust culture of recovery and care within your team, with the goal of restoring (or even growing) strength as well as improved well-being and performance.

PUTTING IT INTO PRACTICE: EXERCISES

- Which of the above self-care practices is missing or inadequate in your life right now?
- Identify one step you can take to add it.
- When will you do this? Where?
- What support will you need?

Well, how did you do? Have you worked through the exercises in the book?

Any new (or renewed) effort that was inspired by this book is beneficial. The goal of this book is to create a path through growth as a leader. For some people, this will all be new information. For others, it's an opportunity to reflect back and see if anything was missed along the way or has been neglected.

In this chapter, we want to evaluate this experience and just celebrate it in some way. Let's jump right in to doing that.

What have you learned through this book? Write down the top three things or the top three lessons that have really stood out to you. Perhaps it was something that came out in the sessions or something that I talked about. Maybe it was something that you experienced through the course of doing an exercise.

What has worked best for you? Of all of the ideas and tips and tricks that I've discussed or introduced to you, what has best supported your growth as a leader?

What will you continue? Of all of the things that we've talked about, what one to three practices are you most likely to continue using or continue doing?

What questions do you have? Were there any questions or unresolved challenges that came up from trying to use these principles or use these exercises? Do you know how you will resolve them? If not, reach out to me at christian@christianmuntean.com. Send me an email that briefly describes the situation you are facing, your best idea for how you might resolve it, and your question for me. I'll respond.

What was most valuable to you about this experience? How will you invest in yourself next? What do you need for your next area of growth that you want to pursue? Is it reading a book? Is it another program like this? Is it hiring a coach? Is it working with me directly as a coach?

ONGOING GROWTH

There are lots of ways we can invest in ourselves. I believe that we always need to invest in ourselves because as leaders, we serve—or lead—out of who we are.

How will you invest in cultivating or building that tool?

The last thing I'd like to ask you to think about is, What's the next goal that you want to pursue?

Maybe it's completing an existing goal that you haven't followed through on. Maybe there's something else. Oftentimes, as people practice the exercises described in this book, their ability to set goals grows. It's almost as if their horizon has moved further out. They can see further than they could before. So what's the next thing that you would like to accomplish as a leader?

I encourage you to do your three daily practices. These are always helpful.

I want to congratulate you for the time that you've put into this. As I often repeat in the book—personal development is leadership development. It's a part of servant leadership to pursue personal growth. Not many leaders make the opportunity for their own growth in this way. You have.

I would love to hear from you and learn how you've benefited from this book or, for that matter, if you have any questions. Feel free to reach out directly. I read and answer my email.

Last, if you would be so kind as to leave a review on Amazon, it would help others find this book.

SELF-ASSESSMENT

We pursue growth the best when we understand our starting point. This assessment helps us gain clarity on where we are now. This helps us identify areas that we may choose to focus on.

Here are two maxims that—if you embrace them—will transform how you lead and manage:

- You can only manage others as well as you manage yourself.
- You will lead out of who you are. How you lead will reflect your core values, preferences, and habits.

In short, how well your team or organization relates to each other, serves your customers, and produces results is a reflection of you.

Different kinds of leadership situations require different skills and approaches. A fire captain needs to dip into a slightly different bag of leadership tools than the coordinator of an arts collaborative. But at the core, *who* the leader is will have a greater impact on the quality of their leadership than the tools they use.

Below is a self-assessment tool. Answer it as honestly as you can. There aren't right or wrong answers. The intent isn't to produce a score. Instead, we want to reveal areas about you and how you approach life that affect how you lead.

If you are like most leaders, you'll discover topics that you hadn't even considered. Use this to identify areas of strength that you can pull from and lean on as well as areas you'd like to grow in.

LEADERSHIP SELF-ASSESSMENT

Rating					
1 Never	2 Rarely	3 Sometimes	4 Often	5 Mostly	6 Always
Questions					Rating
1 **Helpful relationships.** How often do the six to eight people closest to me actively/intentionally challenge me to grow and become a better person?					
2 **Helpful habits.** How often do my daily habits support my growth as a better person and leader?					
3 **How I see myself.** Do I see myself as someone who has been successful, is currently successful, and will be successful in areas of life that I care about?					
4 **How I see others.** How naturally do I see others as being valuable and having potential?					
5 **How I see life.** Do I see life and the community I'm in as providing opportunities for myself and others?					
6 **Priority mastery.** How quickly and easily can I describe my *one* highest priority for the year, quarter, month, week, and day?					
7 **Follow-through.** How consistently do I follow through on my goals and commitments?					
8 **Intensity.** To what degree can I enter into a sustained state of concentrated focus *at will?*					
9 **Patience.** Can I easily wait for others or for results?					

10	**Inspiring a shared vision.** How consistently would those I lead describe me as having inspired a vision that they now share?	
11	**Modeling the way.** How consistently would those I lead say that I model the values and desired behaviors of our organization?	
12	**Empowering others.** How consistently would those I lead say they feel empowered by me to be more and do more?	
13	**Challenging the process.** How consistently would those I lead say they feel as if I appropriately challenge the status quo and practices that don't bring value?	
14	**Encouraging the heart.** How frequently would those I lead say they feel that I encourage and support them?	
15	**Conflict.** How consistently do I intervene in or lead conflicts toward an effective resolution?	
16	**Change.** Am I able to introduce and lead change in a way that will produce maximum value and minimum unhelpful disruption?	
17	**Crisis.** Can I confidently intervene in crises and guide them to a positive (or at least minimally damaging) solution?	
18	**Progress checking.** Do I define expectations and check on progress being made regularly and clearly?	
19	**Endurance.** Am I able to lead long-term initiatives without losing focus or commitment?	
20	**Systems and structures.** Do I ensure that appropriate systems and structures that produce consistency and efficiency are set up and followed?	
21	**Renewing vision.** How often do I revisit and reinvigorate my own sense of vision as well as that of my team?	

| 22 | **Recovery.** How consistently do I take time to rest, recover from stress, and address my own growth and wholeness? | |

EVALUATE YOUR RESULTS

1. Identify one or two strengths (from above) that seem to come most naturally to you.
   a. How do others benefit from those strengths?
   b. How can you lean into those strengths more to bring even greater benefit or value?
2. Identify one low-scoring area that you think has the greatest impact on your leadership.
   a. What are the consequences or effects of not growing or changing in this area?
   b. What are two or three behaviors you can start, stop, or change that will help you grow?
   c. What kind of help or support do you need?

KEEP IT SIMPLE: FOCUS ON ONE THING

In my experience, leaders who attempt to change everything end up overwhelmed and change nothing. Instead, focus on one area you'd like to improve.

ONLY ONE THING?

Yes. Here's the happy why: First off, it's easier, and you are more likely to be able to make meaningful progress with focus. Also, surprisingly to many people, change in one area often generates a systemic impact. For example, improving your priority mastery will have the benefit of reducing stress, increasing productivity, improving focus, mitigating conflict, and so on. Additionally, it will free up energy and bandwidth to better pursue your next goal.

Next, choose a training plan.

THE TRAINING PLANS

To download a free journal to track your progress follow this link: https://
www.christianmuntean.com/train-to-lead-journal/

You'll find the Self-Assessment, training plans and the journal for recording your responses and progress.

INTRODUCTORY TRAINING:

HEALTHY HABITS AND CONDITIONING

Introductory training focuses on the "Healthy Habits" and "Conditioning"
sections of the book. I call it "introductory" because it addresses the very
basic mindsets and habits required to be effective as a leader. All new leaders and most experienced leaders should start here. In fact, many of my
executive coaching clients end up needing to do work in this space before
we can move on to their other goals.

I recommend "stacking" the healthy habits topics as soon as possible.
They don't take a lot of time or effort, they work better together, and you'll
quickly see results. I often give coaching clients 21-day plans where they
experiment with using these habits daily. They all come back confirming
positive results.

Once you have momentum with healthy habits activities, start working through the conditioning exercises. I'd recommend taking at least some time to explore each, even if it is an area of strength. For areas where you feel more of a challenge, spend at least 21 days focusing on the exercises I recommend.

If you find these exercises to your liking and beneficial, I'd encourage you to spend three to four months in this space. Then follow it by a week or so of rest and recovery practices. Then either repeat or move on to Intermediate if you feel ready. This helps you avoid feeling burned out or bored.

Just as in the fitness training, the big or "easy" gains tend to come early. After that, gains tend to be more incremental. Introductory training focuses on these valuable, early gains.

Recommendations and exercises are included at the end of each chapter.

Seven-Week (or 14-Week) Introductory Training Plan

Cycle 1

- 21 days (days 1–21): Healthy habit stacking.
- 21 days (days 22–42): Conditioning. (Pick one topic.)
- 7 days (days 43–49): Active recovery. Focus on one healthy habit to add or improve.

Cycle 2

Repeat the above. If you have made healthy habit stacking an effortless part of your routine, replace it with a conditioning goal to focus on for 21 days.

- 21 days (days 50–71): Healthy habit stacking.
- 21 days (days 72–92): Conditioning. (Pick one topic.)
- 7 days (days 92–98): Recovery. Pick a recovery exercise to focus on for this week.

Continue cycling like this until you have a basic level of familiarity and comfort with healthy habit stacking and conditioning. Don't pursue mastery or perfection. That will come with many reps over time. Focus on progress: being better than you were.

INTERMEDIATE TRAINING: STRENGTH AND POWER

Intermediate training builds on conditioning to focus on strength and power work. Conditioning provides the platform. Strength lets you actually play. Read through all of the five leadership strengths that I describe.

12-Week Training Plan

- Week 1: Healthy habits and conditioning. Pick one area you need to revisit.
- Weeks 2–7: Strength. Pick one strength to focus on.
- Week 8: Active recovery. Pick one healthy habit or conditioning exercise to add or revisit.
- Weeks 9–11: Power. Pick one to focus on.
- Week 12: Recovery. Pick one recovery exercise.

You can cycle through this plan either by revisiting a strength or power area or by focusing on a new one.

ADVANCED TRAINING: ENDURANCE

Advanced training moves from a shorter-term leadership development focus to a lifestyle of leadership growth and excellence. At this point, the leader begins to move into larger macro training schedules. With advanced training, you can start setting larger-growth goals or preparing for major transitions in your responsibilities.

24+ Week Training Plan

Cycle 1

- Week 1: Healthy habits and conditioning. Pick one area you need to revisit.
- Weeks 2–5: Strength. Pick one strength to focus on.

- Week 6: Active recovery. Revisit one healthy habit or conditioning exercise.
- Weeks 7–8: Power. Pick one power exercise.
- Weeks 9–11: Endurance. Pick one endurance exercise.
- Week 12: Recovery. Pick a recovery exercise.

Cycle 2

- Weeks 1–4: Strength. Pick one strength exercise.
- Weeks 5–6: Power. Pick one power exercise.
- Week 7: Active recovery. Pick one healthy habit or conditioning exercise.
- Weeks 8–11: Endurance. Pick one endurance area to focus on.
- Week 12: Recovery. Pick one recovery exercise.

Repeat for as many cycles as you like.

Once you are at the advanced level, you should have a stronger sense of "I need a little more time here," or "I think I've gotten all I can out of that for now." Adjust your training around your goals.

If you know that there is a major transition or challenge coming up, you might want to focus on growth areas that will help your leadership at that time. That may mean adjusting the length of a focus period. Or it could mean addressing two areas of strength or power consecutively.

The general rule of thumb is to work on something *at least* until you start to see growth. Transition when that growth starts to plateau. Get help when you need it.

A thought about periodization—I wrote this book, in part, to answer the question "What one book about leadership do you recommend?" Just as periodization isn't the only way for athletes to train, it isn't the only way for leaders to grow, but it is a structure that works. If you don't know where to start, it'll be a powerful tool for you. If you already have familiarity with leadership development, this will recharge or refocus your growth. It is also very likely to help you address problem areas that are easy to avoid because they are uncomfortable.

ENDNOTES

1   Robert Greenleaf, *Servant Leadership: A Journey into the Nature of Legitimate Power & Greatness* (Mahwah: Paulist Press), 2002.

2   "The Servant as Leader," Robert K. Greenleaf Center for Servant Leadership, accessed October 9, 2023, https://www.greenleaf.org/what-is-servant-leadership/.

3   Om Hemant Patel, "Origins of Servant Leadership," Clearly Agile, accessed October 9, 2023, https://www.clearlyagile.com/agile-blog/origins-of-servant-leadership.

4   "How Robert Greenleaf Created Servant Leadership," Triple Crown Leadership, October 13, 2021, https://triplecrownleadership.com/greenleaf-created-servant-leadership/.

5   Robert Greenleaf, *Servant: Retrospect & Prospect* (New Hampshire: Windy Row Press, 1980), 22.

6   Travis Edwards, "Periodization Training: A Beginner's Guide," Healthline, March 30, 2021, https://www.healthline.com/health/fitness/periodization-training.

7   Anthelme Brillat-Savarin, *Gastronomy as a Fine Art or The Science of Good Living: A Translation of Physiologie du Goût* (London: Chatto & Windus, Piccadilly, 1889), 40.

8   "74 Years of Dedication," Framingham Heart Study, accessed October 9, 2023, https://www.framinghamheartstudy.org/fhs-about/.

9   James H. Fowler and Nicholas A. Christakis, "Dynamic Spread of Happiness in a Large Social Network: Longitudinal Analysis Over 20 Years in the Framingham Heart Study," *British Medical Journal* 337, no. a2338 (2008), https://doi.org/10.1136/bmj.a2338.

10 Nicholas A. Christakis and James H. Fowler, "The Spread of Obesity in a Large Social Network Over 32 Years," *New England Journal of Medicine* 357, no. 4 (2007): 370–379, https://pubmed.ncbi.nlm.nih.gov/17652652/.

11 "How Stress Affects Your Health," American Psychological Associations, last updated October 31, 2022, https://www.apa.org/topics/stress/health.

12 Ellen L. Idler, David A. Boulifard, and Richard J. Contrada, "Mending Broken Hearts: Marriage and Survival Following Cardiac Surgery," *Journal of Health and Social* Behavior 53, no. 1 (2012): 33–49, https://pubmed.ncbi.nlm.nih.gov/22382719/.

13 Koichiro Shiba et al., "Purpose in Life and 8-Year Mortality by Gender and Race/Ethnicity Among Older Adults in the U.S.," *Preventative Medicine* 164, 107310 (2022), https://doi.org/10.1016/j.ypmed.2022.107310.

14 Roma Bhatia et al., "Social Networks, Social Support, and Life Expectancy in Older Adults: The Cardiovascular Health Study," *Archives of Gerontology and Geriatrics* 111, 104981 (2023): https://doi.org/10.1016/j.archger.2023.104981.

15 Walt Wright, "Relational Leadership—Interview with Dr. Walt Wright," Leadership.com.sg, accessed October 9, 2023, http://www.leadership.com.sg/leaders-chat/interviews-with-ceo/interview-with-dr-walt-wright-on-relational-leadership/.

16 Marshall Goldsmith, *What Got You Here Won't Get You There* (New York: Hachette Books, 2007).

17 James Clear, *Atomic Habits: An Easy and Proven Way to Build Good Habits and Break Bad Ones* (New York: Penguin Random House, 2018).

18 Charles Horton Cooley, *On Self and Social Organization* (Chicago: University of Chicago Press, 1998), 22.

19 Charlotte Nickerson, "Looking-Glass Self: Theory, Definition and Examples," Simply Psychology, last updated September 22, 2023, https://www.simplypsychology.org/charles-cooleys-looking-glass-self.html.

20 Dan Sullivan, "How to Grow Your Confidence Every Single Day," Strategic Coach, accessed October 9, 2023, https://resources.strategiccoach.com/the-multiplier-mindset-blog/how-to-grow-your-confidence-every-single-day.

21 Robert Rosenthal and Kermit L. Fode, "The Effect of Experimenter Bias on the Performance of the Albino Rat," *Behavioral Science* 8, no. 3 (1963): 183–189, https://doi.org/10.1002/bs.3830080302.

22 "Experimenter Expectancy Effect," Oxford Reference, accessed October 9, 2023, https://www.oxfordreference.com/view/10.1093/oi/authority.20110803095805141.

23 Olivia Johnston, Helen Wildy, and Jennifer Shand, "A Decade of Teacher Expectations Research 2008–2018: Historical Foundations, New Developments, and Future Pathways," *Australian Journal of Education* 63, no. 1 (2019): 44–73, https://doi.org/10.1177/0004944118824420.

24 Sara Ryding, "What Is a Double-Blind Trial?," News Medical Life Sciences, last updated March 19, 2021, https://www.news-medical.net/health/What-is-a-Double-Blind-Trial.aspx.

25 "Placebo Effect," Better Health Channel, July 23, 2021, https://www.betterhealth.vic.gov.au/health/conditionsandtreatments/placebo-effect.

26 "Placebo Effect," Better Health Channel.

27 "About Me," Viktor Frankl, MD, PhD, accessed October 9, 2023, https://drviktorfrankl.com/.

28 Viktor Frankl, *Man's Search for Meaning* (Boston: Beacon Press, 1959).

29 "2008 Recession: What It Was and What Caused It," Investopedia, last updated April 30, 2023, https://www.investopedia.com/terms/g/great-recession.asp.

30 Zig Ziglar, *See You at the Top*, 25th anniversary ed. (Pelican Publishing, 2000).

31 Theodore Roosevelt to Granville Stanley Hall, November 29, 1899.

32 "What Is Body Conditioning?," Hussle, July 31, 2020, https://www.hussle.com/blog/what-is-body-conditioning/.

33 Linda Poon, "The Rise and Fall of New Year's Fitness Resolutions, in 5 Charts," Bloomberg, January 16, 2019, https://www.bloomberg.com/news/articles/2019-01-16/here-s-how-quickly-people-ditch-weight-loss-resolutions.

34 Christine VanDeVelde, "Carol Dweck: Praising Intelligence: Costs to Children's Self-Esteem and Motivation," Stanford Bing Nursery School, November 1, 2007, https://bingschool.stanford.edu/news/carol-dweck-praising-intelligence-costs-children s-self-esteem-and-motivation.

35 Joseph Stromberg, "Firefighters Do a Lot Less Firefighting than They Used To. Here's What They Do Instead," Vox, last updated February 27, 2015, https://www.vox.com/2014/10/30/7079547/fire-firefighter-decline-medical.

36 Angela L. Duckworth, "Grit: The Power of Passion and Perseverance," TED video, April 2013, 6:00. https://www.ted.com/talks/angela_lee_duckworth_grit_the_power_of_passion_and_perseverance?language=en.

37 "Craig Ballantyne," Early to Rise, accessed October 9, 2023, https://www.earlyto-rise.com/.

38 Casey Meserve, "What Is the Aerobic Heart Rate Zone and How Do You Target It?," Whoop, May 27, 2021, https://www.whoop.com/us/en/thelocker/aerobic-heart-rate-zone/.

39 Mofrad Muntasir, "Continuous Improvement—How to Get 1% Better Every Day from Today," Better Humans, February 18, 2022, https://betterhumans.pub/continuous-improvement-how-to-get-1-better-every-day-from-today-a8128c942c61.

40 Francis de Sales, *Spiritual Maxims* (New York: Harper, 1953), 124.

41 "The Kouzes and Posner Research," LeaderShare, accessed October 10, 2023, https://leadershare.ca/the-kouzes-and-posner-research.

42 Barry Z. Posner and James M. Kouzes, *The Leadership Challenge: How to Get Extraordinary Things Done in Organizations*, 3rd ed. (Hoboken: Jossey-Bass), 2002.

43 Sourya Acharya and Samarth Shukla, "Mirror Neurons: Enigma of the Metaphysical Modular Brain," *Journal of Natural Science, Biology and Medicine* 3, no. 2 (2012): 118–124, https://www.ncbi.nlm.nih.gov/pmc/articles/PMC3510904.

44 Robert Greenleaf, *Servant Leadership: A Journey into the Nature of Legitimate Power and Greatness* (Mahwah: Paulist Press, 1991), 13.

45 James M. Kouzes and Barry Z. Posner, *The Challenge Continues: Participant Workbook* (San Francisco: Wiley, 2010).

46 Jim Collins, "Getting the Right People in the Right Seats Over Time," Jim Collins, accessed October 10, 2023, https://www.jimcollins.com/media_topics/inTheRight-Seats.html.

47 Etymonline, s.v. "encourage (v.)," last updated August 29, 2023, https://www.etymonline.com/word/encourage.

48 Gabrielle Redford, "Amy Edmondson: Psychological Safety Is Critically Important in Medicine," Association of American Medical Colleges, November 12, 2019, https://www.aamc.org/news/amy-edmondson-psychological-safety-critically-important-medicine.

49 Charles Duhigg, "What Google Learned from Its Quest to Build the Perfect Team," *New York Times*, February 25, 2016, https://www.nytimes.com/2016/02/28/magazine/what-google-learned-from-its-quest-to-build-the-perfect-team.html.

50 Mahatma Gandhi, *Young India 1924–1926* (Triplicane: S. Ganesan, 1927), 477.

51 Andrew Zimmerman Jones, "Defining Power in Physics," ThoughtCo, last updated July 15, 2019, https://www.thoughtco.com/power-2699001.

52 Stew Smith, "The Ins and Outs of Air Force Pararescue (PJ) Training," Military.com, accessed October 10, 2023, https://www.military.com/military-fitness/air-force-special-operations/air-force-para-rescue.

53 Bruce T. Blythe, *Blindsided: A Manager's Guide to Crisis Leadership*, 2nd ed. (Red Bank: Rothstein Publishing), 2014.

54 Christopher Klein, "The Sled Dog Relay That Inspired the Iditarod," History.com, last updated May 16, 2023, https://www.history.com/news/the-sled-dog-relay-that-inspired-the-iditarod.

55 Klein, "The Sled Dog Relay."

56 Brian Hickox, "The Red Lantern Award," Iditarod, March 18, 2019, https://iditarod.com/edu/the-red-lantern-award/.

57 "The History of Brazilian Jiu Jitsu," Dark Horse: Brazilian Jiu-Jitsu, January 6, 2023, https://bjjdarkhorse.com/the-history-of-brazilian-jiu-jitsu/.

58 Jose M. Fraguas, *Grappling Masters* (Action Pursuit Group, 2004).

59 Associated Press, "Helio Gracie, Promoter of Jiu-Jitsu, Dies at 95," *New York Times*, January 29, 2009, https://www.nytimes.com/2009/01/30/sports/othersports/30gracie.html.

www.ingramcontent.com/pod-product-compliance
Lightning Source LLC
Chambersburg PA
CBHW021155160726
47994CB00001B/223